LETTER VII:

JOSEPH SMITH AND OLIVER COWDERY EXPLAIN THE HILL CUMORAH

Other LDS nonfiction by Jonathan Neville

The Lost City of Zarahemla
Brought to Light
Moroni's America
Moroni's America (Pocket edition)
Mesomania
The Editors: Joseph, William, and Don Carlos Smith
Whatever Happened to the Golden Plates?
Because of this Theory
Why Mormons Need the Book of Mormon
Moroni's History (2018)

———

LDS fiction by Jonathan Neville

Before the World Finds Out
The Joy Helpers
Moroni's Keys
Among All Nations
In Earthly Things

———

Internet
http://www.lettervii.com/
http://bookofmormonwars.blogspot.com/
http://mormonmesomania.blogspot.com/
http://bookofmormonconsensus.blogspot.com/
http://thefifthmission.blogspot.com/

LETTER VII:

Joseph Smith and Oliver Cowdery Explain the Hill Cumorah

Jonathan Neville, MS, JD

Letter VII: Joseph Smith and Oliver Cowdery Explain the Hill Cumorah

Large Print edition, third printing.

This is a work of nonfiction. The author has made every effort to be accurate and complete and welcomes comments, suggestions, and corrections, which can be emailed to lostzarahemla@gmail.com.

All opinions expressed in this work are the responsibility of the author alone.

ISBN-13: 978-1983541537
ISBN-10: 1983541532

Front cover: View of the Hill Cumorah in western New York, looking northeast from the western side of the valley. The famous statue of Moroni atop the hill is below the *V* in *VII*, slightly to the right. Photo by author.

DIGITAL
LEGEND
Toll Free: 1-877-222-1960

www.digitalegend.com
www.LetMeReadIt.com

To open-minded people everywhere

—>>> <<<—

Note to Readers:

If you've never heard of Letter VII, you're not alone.

However, when Joseph Smith was alive, members of the Church knew Letter VII well. It was the seventh in a series of eight historical letters that Joseph helped Oliver Cowdery write. The letters were republished several times. Joseph included it in his own journal as part of his life story and referenced it in D&C 128.

In our day, few Latter-day Saints have even heard of Letter VII.

Fewer still have read it.

But in the last couple of years, thousands of people have read Letter VII. More are reading it all the time because it addresses issues that are as critical today as they were when it was written in 1835.

In Letter VII, Joseph and Oliver **unequivocally declared** that the Hill Cumorah—the scene of the final battles of the Jaredites and the Nephites and the location of Mormon's depository of Nephite records (Mormon 6:6)—**was in western New York.**

Read Letter VII for yourself and see what you think.

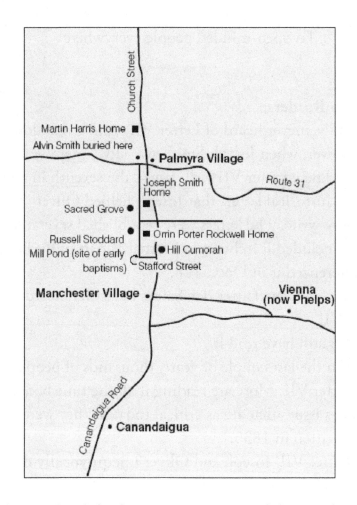

"He [Moroni] said **this history was written and deposited not far from that place…**" Letter VII

Map of Cumorah in proximity to other sites
(Adapted from map on lds.org)

Table of Contents

Figure 1 - Reenactment of translation table

Re-enactment of the table where Joseph Smith and Oliver Cowdery translated the Book of Mormon in Joseph's rebuilt home at the Priesthood Restoration Site in Oakland Township, Pennsylvania (formerly Harmony, PA). Photo by author.

Figure 2 - Oliver Cowdery

Daguerreotype of Oliver Cowdery, taken in the 1840s
by James Presley Ball
found in the Library of Congress

Timeline Summary

April-June 1829. Oliver writes as Joseph dictates the translation of the Book of Mormon from the Harmony plates.

May 1829. Joseph and Oliver receive the Aaronic priesthood from John the Baptist. Later they receive the Melchizedek priesthood from Peter, James and John.

June 1829. Joseph, Oliver, and David Whitmer meet the divine messenger who is taking the Harmony plates to Cumorah. Later the messenger brings the plates of Nephi (the Fayette plates) to Fayette for Joseph to translate.

June 1829. Joseph, Oliver, David and Martin Harris see the plates shown to them by an angel.

1829. Oliver and Joseph visit the room in Cumorah that holds a record depository and other artifacts.

April 1830. The Church is organized. Oliver is named an apostle of Jesus Christ and the second elder of the Church.

Sept. 1830. Oliver and others preach the gospel to the Lamanites in New York, Ohio, and Missouri (D&C 28, 30, 32).

Oct 1834. Joseph helps Oliver write a series of eight letters that will become part of Joseph's history.

5 Dec. 1834. Joseph ordains Oliver Assistant Church President.

July 1835. Oliver publishes **Letter VII** in the *Messenger and Advocate.*

October 1835. Joseph's scribes copy President Cowdery's letters, including **Letter VII**, into his journal as part of "a history of my life."

April 3, 1836. The Lord appears to Joseph and Oliver in the Kirtland temple, along with Moses, Elias, and Elijah.

October 1840. Parley P. Pratt republishes **Letter VII** in the *Millennial Star* in England.

March 1841. With Joseph's encouragement, Benjamin Winchester republishes **Letter VII** in the *Gospel Reflector.*

April 1841. With Joseph's encouragement, Don Carlos republishes **Letter VII** letter in the *Times and Seasons.*

February 1844. **Letter VII** republished in a pamphlet in England.

June 1844. William Smith republishes **Letter VII** letter in *The Prophet,* the Mormon newspaper in New York City, two days after the martyrdom in Carthage.

1899. **Letter VII** is published in Utah in the *Improvement Era.*

Chapter 1 – Cumorah Controversy

Many members of the Church are surprised to learn there is a controversy about the location of the Hill Cumorah. Most of us think it's in New York, a few miles south of Palmyra.

It's obvious, right?

Joseph got the plates there. The Jaredites and Nephites died there. Mormon's depository was there. (Mormon 6:6)

How could the Hill Cumorah *not* be in New York?

Believe it or not, many LDS Book of Mormon scholars and educators say the Hill Cumorah is *not* in New York.

They insist the Hill Cumorah is in *Central America!*

They have been teaching this idea at BYU and in CES (the Church Educational System) for years.

Many LDS people become confused when they learn what these scholars teach. If Moroni buried the plates in New York, how could Cumorah be in Central America?

The scholars have an explanation. They call it the "two-Cumorahs" theory. They say the "hill in New York" is merely the place where Joseph found the plates, while the "real hill Cumorah" is somewhere in southern Mexico.

In 1936, when some LDS scholars first began accepting the two-Cumorahs theory, Apostle and Church Historian Joseph Fielding Smith warned the Saints. "Because of this theory," he wrote, "some members of the Church have become **confused and greatly disturbed** in their faith in the Book of Mormon." Twenty years later, as President of the Quorum of the Twelve, President Smith repeated the warning in his book, *Doctrines of Salvation.*

The fact that the two-Cumorahs theory has become the consensus among many LDS scholars and educators is the reason everyone in the Church needs to read Letter VII and learn what the prophets and apostles have taught about the New York Cumorah.

I clarify at the outset that I have great respect for LDS scholars and educators, including those who focus on the Book of Mormon. They are faithful members of the Church. They work hard and follow accepted academic principles and practices. I'm not criticizing them personally or accusing them of anything untoward.

In fact, on its face, the two-Cumorahs theory is not irrational. It is the product of careful analysis of the Book of Mormon text. But it has a major, devastating flaw.

This theory repudiates Letter VII and every prophet and apostle who has affirmed it, including members of the First Presidency speaking in General Conference.

-->>> <<<-

When Joseph Smith was alive, everyone knew that Cumorah was in New York because Letter VII said it was.

Letter VII was one of eight essays about Church history that Oliver Cowdery wrote with the assistance of Joseph Smith. As was customary in those days, the essays were published in the Church newspaper in Kirtland, the *Messenger and Advocate,* as letters addressed to W.W. Phelps. The essays provided details about the restoration of the Priesthood, Moroni's visit to Joseph, and the Hill Cumorah.

In Letter VII, President Cowdery wrote:

At about one mile west [of Cumorah] rises another ridge of less height, running parallel with the former, leaving a beautiful vale between. ...when one reflects on the fact, that here, between these hills, the entire power and national strength of both the Jaredites and Nephites were destroyed.

There is no ambiguity, hesitation, or speculation. President Cowdery declares that, *in fact*, the New York Cumorah is the site of the final battles.

Letter VII was published in five Church newspapers during Joseph's lifetime. Joseph included it in his history (*History* 1834-1836), where you can read it in the Joseph Smith Papers today. (Just go to josephsmithpaper.org and type "Letter VII" in the search box.) No one questioned the New York setting. So how did we end up with a "two-Cumorahs" theory that has become the consensus among certain LDS scholars and educators?

-→≫ ≪←-

Joseph Smith never varied from or questioned Letter VII. *Everything* that can be directly linked to him supports the New York setting; *nothing* that supports a setting outside New York can be directly linked to him.

Other Mormon authors, such as Parley P. Pratt and his brother Orson Pratt, recognized that most people in the world expected to have physical evidence of the authenticity of the Book of Mormon before they would accept and read the book.

Because they knew Cumorah was in New York, but the most famous and exciting ancient ruins were in Central and South America, these authors developed a theory that the Book of

Mormon described the history of the entire hemisphere. This led some (but never Joseph Smith) to advocate that (i) Lehi landed in Chile, (ii) the Lamanites inhabited South America (the "land southward"), Panama was the narrow neck of land, and the Nephites inhabited North America (the "land northward").

Others speculated that Lehi landed in Panama or somewhere else in Central America.

Most notoriously, anonymous articles published in the 1842 *Times and Seasons* claimed that Mayan ruins were Nephite. Zarahemla was identified in Guatemala.[1]

But about Cumorah, there was no speculation. Regardless of other ideas, Cumorah was absolutely, unquestionably in New York. The New York Cumorah has been consistently taught by LDS prophets, including members of the First Presidency in General Conference, through the 1970s.

Beginning in the 1920s, certain scholars developed a "limited geography" theory that placed Book of Mormon events in Central America (Mesoamerica). They calculated that the narrative took place within about an 800-mile radius of locations in Central America. The hill in New York—3,400 miles from Guatemala—was considered too far away to be the Book of Mormon Cumorah.

Book of Mormon scholars had to choose between a New York Cumorah and a Guatemalan Zarahemla.

They made their choice.

The problem is they *rejected the New York Cumorah* in favor of the theoretical sites in Central America.

---

[1] In my books *The Lost City of Zarahemla, Brought to Light,* and *The Editors: Joseph, William and Don Carlos Smith,* I present detailed historical evidence that shows Joseph had nothing to do with these anonymous editorials.

-→⋙ ⋘←-

Here's how the scholars rationalized the decision to accept Central America and reject New York.

They decided that the hill in New York was named Cumorah solely because Joseph obtained the plates there—not because it was the hill mentioned in the text (Mormon 6:6). They think (i) the name Cumorah was attached to the hill by tradition, (ii) Letter VII solidified the false tradition, and (iii) Joseph Smith passively accepted it.

The intellectuals think the "real" Cumorah—the scene of the final battles of the Jaredites and the Nephites and the location of Mormon's depository—is in Central America.

In their view, they were vindicating what Joseph taught in 1842 because they assumed that he wrote or approved of the anonymous *Times and Seasons* articles. They concluded he changed his mind about Cumorah because of a popular illustrated book about ruins in Central America.

These LDS scholars have spent decades looking for evidence in Central America. They have written dozens of papers and books about illusory "correspondences" between Mayan civilization and what they read in the text, a process they call "finding Mesoamerica in the text."

One prominent group that includes many LDS scholars (and even emeritus General Authorities) has declared its mission is "to increase understanding of the Book of Mormon as an ancient Mesoamerican document."

By the 1980s, the Mesoamerican/two-Cumorahs theory was popular enough to appear in the *Ensign* magazine.

This theory now permeates Church literature, art, media, and even lesson manuals. Mesoamerican imagery is imprinted on the minds of anyone who has grown up in the Church or been educated by CES. Millions of copies of the Book of Mormon have been published with the Arnold Friberg paintings depicting Central American locations.

There is an interesting aspect of the Friberg paintings that is often overlooked. He actually painted Mormon and Moroni together on the hill Cumorah—in New York.

Until 1981, this painting was included in the blue missionary editions of the Book of Mormon. It reflected a geography extending from the New York Cumorah to Central America (at least).

This painting depicts the teachings of the prophets and apostles about the New York Cumorah, including Letter VII.

But in 1981, this Cumorah painting was *replaced* with the painting of Moroni, alone, at the hill in New York, burying the plates.

The message: Moroni's hill is not Cumorah.

Chapter 2 – Rejecting Letter VII

Oliver Cowdery wrote these eight historical essays with the assistance of Joseph Smith in 1834-1835. They were published as letters to W.W. Phelps, beginning in October 1834.

Why October1834?

In October 1834, an influential anti-Mormon book titled *Mormonism Unvailed* [sic] was published in Painesville, Ohio, just a few miles from Kirtland. The book attacked the character of Joseph Smith and his family. It also established the theory that Joseph (and/or others) created the Book of Mormon by copying from an unpublished book by Solomon Spaulding.

Oliver responded to these claims by citing facts.

To counter the argument that the Book of Mormon was fiction based on Spaulding's book, Oliver declared in Letter VII that it was a fact that the final battles of the Nephites and Jaredites was in the mile-wide valley west of the Hill Cumorah in New York.

Anti-Mormons reject the claims of Letter VII.

And so do many LDS scholars and educators today.

LDS scholars are not unaware of Letter VII.

They reject Letter VII by rationalizing that neither Oliver Cowdery nor Joseph Smith *claimed* to receive revelation about where the final battles took place.

Therefore, according to the scholars, they did not receive revelation about Cumorah.

Therefore, Oliver was merely speculating (or repeating a tradition created by unknown persons). But he was wrong, and so was Joseph Smith, because modern scholars know more about Cumorah than Joseph and Oliver did.

--->>> <<<---

The logical fallacy here is obvious. There is no reason to believe that Joseph and Oliver wrote down every revelation they ever had, or that everything they wrote down survived to the present day. When they asserted that something was a *fact*, as they did in Letter VII, the burden of proof is on those who claim they were actually *speculating*—and thereby created a false tradition that misled the Church for decades, until the scholars corrected them.

Notice, the two-Cumorahs theory also creates a slippery slope problem. It requires that Letter VII be factually wrong. But if Oliver Cowdery and Joseph Smith were speculating about important things they stated were facts, then why should we believe other things they said were facts? After all, Oliver's letters also describe the visit of John the Baptist and other important events.

In my view, the scholars' rejection of Letter VII's statement of fact is tantamount to the basic anti-Mormon argument that Oliver and Joseph made up everything.

Almost as bad is the notion that we can only distinguish between what Joseph and Oliver *knew* and what they *invented* by asking modern scholars to decide what is true.

This isn't to say that Oliver and Joseph were perfect. Both admitted weaknesses and dealt with them. But both were adamant that the things they claimed happened really happened, and that the revelations were true.

--->>> <<<---

Each of us views the world through our own filters. We have biases. Think about your own biases as you read this (or any other) book. Consider the biases of the author.

Here is my bias. You can agree or disagree, but you should know that this is the filter I use to assess the facts.

I think Joseph Smith and Oliver Cowdery were credible and reliable witnesses. I think they were truthful. I don't think they would say something was a fact unless they knew it was. (Later in this chapter I'll explain how they knew Cumorah was in New York.)

Because Joseph and Oliver worked together on these letters, and because Joseph endorsed them repeatedly after they were published, I consider these letters, including Letter VII, as the testimony of two witnesses.

Their dual witness is the foundation of our beliefs about the restoration of Priesthood keys, the translation of the Book of Mormon, and more. Letter VII is no different.

My bias extends to all the prophets and apostles who have affirmed Letter VII's teaching about Cumorah in New York, including members of the First Presidency speaking in General Conference.

Scholars and educators who reject Letter VII have a different bias. Because they believe Joseph and Oliver were wrong, they think Letter VII deserves no deference. They think every prophet and apostle who has taught that Cumorah is in New York was perpetrating a false tradition.

Keep these distinct biases in mind as you read the rest of this book, as well as any book on the topic. Ask which bias more closely reflects your own bias.

-⇒≫ ≪⇐-

In these historical letters, Oliver clearly distinguished between fact and speculation. As a school teacher and future lawyer, he knew the difference. He had a reputation for integrity and honesty.

Plus, he acted on his knowledge.

Within a few months of transcribing the entire text of the Book of Mormon—he wrote most of the Original and Printer's Manuscripts—and overseeing the printing, Oliver walked hundreds of miles in the winter from New York to Missouri, sometimes through three feet of snow, to preach the gospel to the Lamanites.

Would he do that if he was making things up?

Oliver faced a series of extremely difficult challenges in the early days of the Church, but he remained faithful to his testimony of the Book of Mormon and the things he had written. He left the Church for a time under circumstances that remain unclear, but after Joseph died, Oliver was rebaptized. He intended to join the Saints in Utah. On his way, he stopped in Missouri to visit his friend and brother-in-law, David Whitmer, another of the Three Witnesses. While there, Oliver died of an illness.

The fact that Joseph approved republication of Letter VII multiple times *even while Oliver was outside the Church* attests to its importance and veracity.

In fact, scholars have long relied on Oliver's series of eight letters about Church history. Portions of Letter I are found in the Pearl of Great Price today. Oliver provided valuable, unique details about Moroni's first visit to Joseph Smith and the construction of the stone box.

--->>> <<<---

There is another very important aspect of Cumorah that has been largely ignored.

Let's assume for a moment that the scholars are correct; i.e., because Joseph and Oliver never claimed to receive a revelation about the site of the final battles, they *did not* receive such a revelation. (I realize the conclusion doesn't follow—in the spirit of Alma 12:9, people receive revelation all the time that they don't discuss—but let's consider the scholars' argument anyway.)

Everyone who accepts Joseph as a Prophet agrees that he obtained the plates from a box Moroni made of stone and cement in the New York Hill Cumorah around 421 A.D. There is extrinsic evidence to corroborate Joseph's story, such as other people who saw the box and the plates.

But Joseph and Oliver also visited a room in the same hill that contained many other plates and artifacts. In Letter VII, Oliver said the depository was in the same New York hill where Joseph found the plates.

There are nine separate accounts relating aspects of these visits. The most detailed account was given by Brigham Young in a sermon he preached just two months before he died. He pointed out that Oliver Cowdery did not talk about such things in meetings, but he did privately.

Brigham said:

Oliver Cowdery went with the Prophet Joseph when he deposited these plates. Joseph did not translate all of the plates; there was a portion of them sealed… When Joseph got the plates, the angel instructed him to carry them back to the hill Cumorah, which he did.

Oliver says that when Joseph and Oliver went there, the hill opened, and they walked into a cave, in which there was a large and spacious room… They laid the plates on a table; it was a large table that stood in the room. Under this table there was a pile of plates as much as two feet high, and there were altogether in this room more plates than probably many wagon loads; they were piled up in the corners and along the walls.[2]

Wilford Woodruff said Joseph did not return to the box but went into a "cave" in the Hill Cumorah with Oliver Cowdery and deposited those plates upon a table or shelf. Other accounts described the room as 16 feet square and 15 feet high. The room contained more artifacts "than a six-mule team could draw," "more than ten men could carry."

--->>> <<<--

Mormon himself, in Mormon 6:6, says he "hid up in the hill Cumorah all the records which had been entrusted to me by the hand of the Lord, save it were these few plates which I gave unto my son Moroni."

There are three possibilities.

1. Mormon hid the plates in the New York Cumorah and Joseph and Oliver visited the repository as Brigham Young and others said.

2. Mormon hid the plates in a hill Cumorah somewhere else—say, Guatemala or Peru—and Joseph and Oliver merely had a visionary experience of some sort.

3. Joseph and Oliver never visited any such room and the accounts by Brigham Young, Wilford Woodruff, and others consisted of fables or traditions.

Let's take them in reverse order.

--->>> <<<--

---

[2] *Journal of Discourses*, vol. 19, pp. 36-45.

3. It is true that all of the accounts of the room in the hill are hearsay; i.e., we have nothing in writing directly from Joseph or Oliver that describes their visits to the repository. However, in Letter VII President Cowdery declared the depository was in the same Hill Cumorah where Joseph found the plates. Although he didn't explain how he knew this to be the case, he told Brigham Young that he had visited the depository with Joseph.

The people who knew Oliver and Joseph best, including Brigham Young, Wilford Woodruff, and Heber C. Kimball, did believe Letter VII, just as they believed Oliver's account of visiting the depository and his testimony as one of the Three Witnesses of the Book of Mormon.

In D&C 28:1, dated September 1830, the Lord said, "Behold, I say unto thee, Oliver, that it shall be given unto thee that thou shalt be heard by the church in all things whatsoever thou shalt teach them by the Comforter, concerning the revelations and commandments which I have given."

In July 1835, Oliver was the ordained Assistant President of the Church. He wrote the historical letters with Joseph Smith's assistance and expected readers—at least, faithful members of the Church—to believe him.

2. LDS scholars have long attributed the accounts related by Brigham Young, Wilford Woodruff, Heber C. Kimball, Orson Pratt, and others to a purely visionary experience; i.e., Joseph, Oliver and others merely had a vision of a hill in Mexico, a vision that was repeated multiple times.

The scholars cite a portion of one of Heber C. Kimball's statements: "the *vision* that Joseph and others had, when they went into a cave in the hill Cumorah, and saw more records than ten men could carry." But the term "vision" is not limited to a spiritual experience; the word can refer to anything which is the object of sight, as in, "the *view* that Joseph and others had, when they went into a cave..."

All of the other accounts are matter-of-fact recitations of actual events, with detailed descriptions. Brigham Young prefaced his remarks by observing how familiar he was with that part of New York. He related the account shortly before he died, when he was in the process of reorganizing the Priesthood throughout the Church. He said he was concerned that Oliver's teaching about the depository would be forgotten if he didn't relate it.

It does not seem to have occurred to Brigham that modern LDS scholars would transform his teaching into a spiritual vision of a hill in Mexico, let alone a spiritual vision shared by multiple people on multiple occasions.

The other reason LDS scholars insist this had to be a purely visionary experience is because the New York hill is a glacial moraine, and a natural cave cannot form in such a geological feature. Even if that's an accurate statement of geology, no one said this was a *natural* cave. According to the 1828 Webster's dictionary, a cave is simply a "hollow place in the earth... this may be natural or artificial."

Brigham and others described a man-made room.

Some years ago a man-made room was reportedly discovered on the west side of the northern end of the Hill Cumorah, not far from the Moroni statue. The walls are made of cut stone and the dimensions match the description reported by Oliver. Even if this stone-walled room is not the one Joseph and Oliver visited, it demonstrates that such a room can exist in the hill.

1. If Brigham Young and the others accurately reported what Oliver said, and if Oliver was telling the truth, then Mormon's depository was in the New York Cumorah.

My bias is in favor of the veracity and reliability of these men. I accept what they taught.

-->>> <<<--

Let's say, hypothetically, that the room discovered in the New York hill is the one Joseph and Oliver visited.

It was empty.

But this is no surprise to Church historians.

When asked about the plates, David Whitmer said they were in a cave. "Where is that cave?" "In the state of New York." "In the Hill of Comorah?" [sic] "No, but not far away from that place."

David also said that "when they [the additional plates] are translated much useful information will be brought to light. But till that day arrives, no Rochester adventurers shall ever see them or the treasures."[3]

Oliver Cowdery also said the plates were no longer in Cumorah. (Letter VII)

I think Joseph, Oliver, Don Carlos, Hyrum, and others moved the Nephite records to another location. That's why they went to the depository, and why Brigham referred to wagon loads of plates, Heber said there were more plates than ten men could carry, etc.

This answer reconciles numerous otherwise inexplicable incidents in Church history. Here's what I think happened.

---

[3] For citations and a more complete explanation of these events, see my book *Whatever Happened to the Golden Plates?*

Joseph translated the plates he obtained from Moroni—the plates he later referred to as the "Original Book of Mormon"—in Harmony, Pennsylvania. He started in 1828 with the Book of Lehi (the 116 pages that Martin Harris lost). He resumed in 1829 with Oliver Cowdery, translating from Mosiah through Moroni. Finally, they translated the Title Page, which was on the last leaf of the plates.

Pursuant to a commandment Joseph received through the Urim and Thummim, Joseph and Oliver wrote to David Whitmer, asking him to come to pick them up and take them to David's father's farm in Fayette, New York. Before they left Harmony, Joseph gave the plates to a heavenly messenger as instructed.

Along the way to Fayette, they encountered a man wearing a knapsack. David offered him a ride but the man said, "No, I am going to Cumorah." David had not heard the name before. He looked to Joseph for an explanation. Joseph said it was the messenger who had the plates.

The messenger's rejection of David's offer makes no sense if he was taking the Harmony plates to Fayette.

Instead, I think the messenger was taking the plates of Mormon (the Harmony plates) to the depository in Cumorah *because Joseph was finished with those plates.*

The Lord had told Joseph in D&C 10 that he would have to translate the "plates of Nephi." The key point to realize: *Joseph did not have the plates of Nephi in Harmony.* We can tell this from the Title Page, which refers to no original plates.

The messenger left the Harmony plates in the depository in Cumorah and picked up the original "plates of Nephi." He took these to Fayette, where Joseph translated them as 1 Nephi through Words of Mormon.

This is a new concept to many Church members, but it is the best explanation for what are otherwise anomalous events in Church history. With this explanation, we no longer have to attribute so many statements of prophets and apostles to error, confusion, or imagination.

-->>> <<<-

Mormon's depository in New York explains other accounts. For example, the Three Witnesses testified they saw the angel turn the plates, but they did not touch them at the time. Joseph told his mother he was relieved that finally other people saw the plates. Yet later, all three witnesses claimed they touched the plates.

When did that happen?

D&C 17:1 promises the witnesses that they "shall have a view of the plates, and also of the breastplate, the sword of Laban, the Urim and Thummim," and the Liahona. However, the Testimony of the Three Witnesses mentions only the plates. I think that statement is accurate and complete. If it is, how do we explain D&C 17:1?

The descriptions of the depository related by Brigham Young, Wilford Woodruff and others included the sword of Laban, the Liahona, and the other objects.

Look again at D&C 17:1. It does not promise that they would see everything simultaneously. Notice how the Lord said they would have a view of the plates, *and also* of the other items. That phrase sets the other objects apart from the plates. I think the Three Witnesses saw these objects on a later occasion, when they visited the depository in Cumorah as Brigham and the others explained.

However, years later David Whitmer when described his experience as one of the Three Witnesses, he said. "We not only saw the plates of the B[ook] of M[ormon] but also the Brass plates, the Plates of the Book of ether, the Plates containing the Record of the wickedness of the people of the world, and many other plates."

According to a note in the Joseph Smith Papers, "he also described a table holding the sword of Laban, the Liahona, and the interpreters, all of which were objects mentioned in the Book of Mormon translation and which a previous revelation had promised the witnesses they would see."[4]

One possibility is that the angel magically transported these items to New York from Central America. I have a bias against magical thinking. If magical transportation was an option, why would Moroni bury the plates in New York for 1400 years? Why did Mormon worry about physically transporting the Nephite records to Cumorah in the first place? (Mormon 4:23)

Another possibility is that the angel brought the items to Fayette from the Cumorah depository along with the plates of Nephi. But that doesn't explain why the Testimony of the Three Witnesses doesn't mention these other items.

I think David was relating what he saw in the depository. I explain my reasoning in my book *Whatever Happened to the Golden Plates?* Because he wasn't supposed to talk about the depository (remember, Oliver didn't discuss it publicly), David conflated his experience in the depository with the Three Witnesses account.

It's also interesting to note that the eight witnesses were in the Palmyra area and only saw one set of plates. Joseph's mother said he got this set of plates from one of the Three Nephites, which is consistent with his having received this set of plates in Fayette from the messenger.

---

[4] http://www.josephsmithpapers.org/paperSummary/appendix-4-testimony-of-three-witnesses-late-june-1829.

Joseph received the Harmony plates from Moroni, not from one of the Three Nephites.

This is why I think Joseph and Oliver, with the assistance of Joseph's brothers Hyrum and Don Carlos and others, moved the plates and artifacts from Cumorah to another location. Whether Joseph and the others told anyone *where* they hid the plates remains an open question.

In April 1928 General Conference, President Ivins said:

Whether they have been removed from the spot where Mormon deposited them we cannot tell, but this we know, that they are safe under the guardianship of the Lord, and that they will be brought forth at the proper time, as the Lord has declared they should be, for the benefit and blessing of the people of the world, for his word never fails.

Did he mean he *could not tell* because he didn't know for sure, or he *could not tell* because he wasn't supposed to?

Is there still a Cumorah controversy?

As long as the two-Cumorahs theory prevails among many LDS scholars and educators, the answer is yes.

To paraphrase Joseph Fielding Smith, thoughtful readers of the Book of Mormon will be *confused* as long as they have to choose between a Hill Cumorah in New York and a Hill Cumorah somewhere else.

Many members of the Church are *greatly disturbed* in their faith of the Book of Mormon when they realize that prominent LDS scholars and educators reject Oliver Cowdery's statements of fact about the Hill Cumorah.

LDS scholars also reject David Whitmer's statements about the messenger on the side of the road who referred to Cumorah. David had lived in that part of New York, but he had never heard of Cumorah. This was the first time he heard the term, so it was memorable for him.

It's one thing for members to become confused about the Book of Mormon because of the two-Cumorahs theory, but think about non-members.

People investigating the Church often search the Internet. They quickly learn about the confusion produced by LDS scholars who reject what Joseph and Oliver wrote in Letter VII about the Hill Cumorah in New York.

Missionaries ask investigators to believe the Testimony of the Three Witnesses. But what are investigators to think when they learn that many LDS scholars and educators reject what two of the Three Witnesses said?

What are the *missionaries* supposed to think?

-➤≫ ≪◄-

Rejecting Letter VII is a serious mistake.

But maybe worse is having members and missionaries who don't even know about Letter VII, or what it says.

Because you're reading this book, you're learning about Letter VII, possibly for the first time.

If you're inclined to reject Letter VII, that's your right. But you should make an informed decision.

And that means understanding the background and context of the letters, as well as their content.

Chapter 3 – Background on Oliver Cowdery

Oliver Cowdery was well qualified to write about the Book of Mormon and early Church history. No one other than Joseph Smith himself was *more* qualified. And Joseph helped Oliver write these eight historical letters.

Oliver and Joseph shared the following experiences (an annotated timeline is included in Appendix I).

1. Received revelations (D&C 6&7)
2. Translated/recorded the Book of Mormon.
3. Received the Aaronic Priesthood from John the Baptist.
4. Received the Melchizedek Priesthood from Peter, James, and John.
5. Ordained and baptized one another.
6. Handled the plates.
7. Visited the repository of Nephite records in the Hill Cumorah.
8. Translated/recorded the Book of Moses
9. Received visits from Moroni, Moses, Elias, Elijah, and the Lord Himself.

Historian Richard Bushman observed, "There is doubtless a theological reason for Oliver participating in some of the most striking revelations of the Restoration—the need for a second witness."[5]

As Assistant President of the Church, Oliver Cowdery was called to act as a spokesman. Notes from the meeting at which he was ordained in December 1834 explain that:

---

[5] Richard L. Bushman, "Oliver's Joseph," in *Days Never to be Forgotten: Oliver Cowdery*, Alexander I. Baugh, Editor (Deseret Book 2009), p.2.

"The office of Assistant President is to assist in presiding over the whole Church, and to officiate in the absence of the President, according to his rank and appointment, viz: President Cowdery, first; President Rigdon Second, and President Williams Third, as they were severally called. The office of this priesthood **is also to act as spokesman**, taking Aaron for an example. The virtue of the above priesthood is to hold the keys of the kingdom of heaven or of the Church..."[6]

A few months after finishing the historical letters, on April 3, 1836, Joseph and Oliver, together, received Priesthood keys from Moses, Elijah, Elias, and the Lord Himself. (D&C 110)

In January, 1841, Joseph ordained Hyrum as Assistant President, pursuant to D&C 124:94-5, which gives an additional explanation of the role Oliver fulfilled in that position:

"I appoint unto him [Hyrum] that he may be a prophet, and a seer, and a revelator unto my church, as well as my servant Joseph; That he may act in concert also with my servant Joseph; and that he shall receive counsel from my servant Joseph... and be crowned with the same blessing, and glory, and honor, and priesthood, and gifts of the priesthood, that once were put upon him that was my servant Oliver Cowdery."

Oliver died on March 3, 1850, in Richmond, Missouri, still faithful to his testimony of the Book of Mormon.

---

[6] http://www.josephsmithpapers.org/paper-summary/account-of-meetings-revelation-and-blessing-5-6-december-1834/1

Chapter 4 – Background on the Eight Historical Letters

In response to Oliver's desire to learn from the Lord, Joseph Smith received a revelation: "I speak unto you [Oliver and David Whitmer], even as unto Paul mine apostle, for you are called even with that same calling with which he was called." (D&C 18:9). The message was suited to Oliver, for like Paul of old, Oliver was a prolific writer.

He was also the "second elder" in the Church (D&C 20:3-4) and an "apostle," so called when he was named "the first preacher of this church unto the church, and before the world." (D&C 21:10, 12).

Oliver was promised that the Church would hear him. "Behold, I say unto thee, Oliver, that it shall be given unto thee that **thou shalt be heard by the church in all things whatsoever thou shalt teach them by the Comforter,** concerning the revelations and commandments which I have given," but he was to write not "by way of commandment, but by wisdom." (D&C 28: 1, 5). Today, an excerpt from Letter I is included in the Pearl of Great Price as a note to Joseph Smith—History.

-→≫ ≪←-

In the early 1830s, Oliver served missions and helped W.W. Phelps establish a Church printing office in Jackson County, Missouri. He took the revelations from Kirtland to Missouri to be printed. In April 1834, he and Fredrick G. Williams were given stewardship over the printing office in Kirtland, Ohio. It was in this role that Oliver published eight letters about Church history—including Letter VII.

Oliver introduced the letters in the first issue of the *Messenger and Advocate*, October 1834 with this plan:

The following communication was designed to have been published in the last No. of the Star;[7] but owing to a press of other matter it was laid over for this No. of the Messenger and Advocate. Since it was written, upon further reflection, we have thought that a full history of the rise of the church of the Latter Day Saints, and the most interesting parts of its progress, to the present time, would be worthy the perusal of the Saints.-If circumstances admit, an article on this subject will appear in each subsequent No. of the Messenger and Advocate, until the time when the church was driven from Jackson Co. Mo. by a lawless banditti; & such other remarks as may be thought appropriate and interesting.

That our narrative may be correct, and particularly the introduction, it is proper to inform our patrons, that our brother J. SMITH jr. has offered to assist us. Indeed, there are many items connected with the fore part of this subject that render his labor indispensable. With his labor and with authentic documents now in our possession, we hope to render this a pleasing and agreeable narrative, well worth the examination and perusal of the Saints.-To do justice to this subject will require time and space: we therefore ask the forbearance of our readers, **assuring them that it shall be founded upon facts.** (emphasis added)

---

[7] This refers to the *Evening and the Morning Star*, the paper that was first published in Independence but then moved to Kirtland when the Missourians destroyed the printing press.

The letters were originally published in the Kirtland-based *Messenger and Advocate* in 1834-1835 as follows:

Letter I – October 1834, *M&A*, vol. I, no. 1
Letter II – November 1834, *M&A*, vol. I, no. 2
Letter III – December 1834, *M&A*, vol. I, no. 3
Letter IV – February 1835, *M&A*, vol. I, no. 5
Letter V – March 1835, *M&A*, vol. I, no. 6
Letter VI – April 1835, *M&A*, vol. I, no. 7
Letter VII – July 1835, *M&A*, vol. I, no. 10
Letter VIII – October 1835, *M&A*, vol. II, no. 1

As mentioned in Chapter 2, the anti-Mormon book *Mormonism Unvailed* [sic] was published in Painesville, Ohio, in October 1834 by Eber D. Howe, editor of the *Painesville Telegraph*. Painesville is located about ten miles northeast of Kirtland. Howe's book contained derogatory affidavits from Joseph's former neighbors in New York and Pennsylvania and a claim that the Book of Mormon was stolen from an unpublished book by Solomon Spaulding.

The eight letters responded to the charges. Oliver emphasized the factual nature of his accounts to contrast with the unfounded allegations of *Mormonism Unvailed*.

Richard Bushman explains the significance of these eight letters.

This was the first published account of Joseph's "marvelous experience" and one of three major sources dealing with his early years along with Lucy Smith's *Biographical Sketches* and Joseph's own manuscript history. Joseph wrote a brief history in 1832 but did not publish it. His longer account was not begun until 1838. Lucy's narrative was dictated after the Prophet's death. Thus, for a number of years, Oliver's account stood alone.[8]

Although Oliver planned to provide "a full history," John Whitmer had been called as the official Church historian to replace Oliver. That made sense going forward; Oliver was busy with the newspaper and likely didn't have time to assemble and keep current whatever important documents were available. But if John Whitmer was going to write about prior Church history—particularly the foundational events—he would have to go to Oliver and Joseph for the information. It made more sense to have Oliver simply write about those events, which is exactly what he did.

John Welch gives additional insight into the process, noting that even after Whitmer replaced Oliver as historian,

> Cowdery continued to act as a historian. He was the only person other than Joseph Smith with firsthand knowledge of many of the founding events of the Restoration. Thus, it was only natural for him to write columns about the history of the Palmyra period of the Church.
>
> Joseph Smith fully supported Cowdery's efforts to publish his history and even offered to assist him with it. Cowdery said that Joseph Smith's labor on the project and "authentic documents now in our possession" would give him the ability to write a historical narrative that was "pleasing and agreeable" to his readers. Would that we had all the documents Cowdery was working from, as documents from the early years of the Church are so rare....
>
> Cowdery's history is invaluable because it contains details that are unique to it, and it is much more detailed than those accounts left by

---

[8] Bushman, op cit., p. 6.

the Prophet himself. But because Cowdery writes that Joseph assisted him with the writing of this history, the division between Cowdery's and Joseph's versions may be a false construct.[9]

Joseph considered President Cowdery's letters part of his own history. On 29 Oct. 1835, his journal entry notes:

"Br W. Parish [Warren Parrish] commenced writing for me… my scribe commenced writing in my journal a history of my life, concluding President [Oliver] Cowdery 2d letter to W.W. Phelps, which president Williams had begun."[10]

Letter VII appears on page 79 of what is now called *History 1834-1836*.[11] Frederick G. Williams, Second Counselor in the First Presidency, began the transcription, but Warren Parrish completed it.

Joseph Smith's *History 1834-1836* is a composite of several records in addition to President Cowdery's letters, including a revised version of Joseph's daily journal entries between September 1835 and January 1836. The history ends on 18 January 1836.

––––––––––––––––––––

[9] John W. Welch, "Oliver Cowdery as Editor, Defender, and Justice of the Peace in Kirtland," in *Days Never to be Forgotten: Oliver Cowdery*, Alexander I. Baugh, Editor (Deseret Book 2009), p.263-4.

[10] *Journal, 1835-1836*, in *The Joseph Smith Papers, Journals, Volume 1: 1832-1839*, p. 76-77. A digital version is available online here: http://josephsmithpapers.org/paperSummary/?target=JSPPJ1_d1e14445#!/paperSumma ry/journal-1835-1836&p=11

[11] *History, 1834-1836*, in *The Joseph Smith Papers, Histories, Volume 1: Joseph Smith Histories*, 1832-1844, pp. 72-79. A digital version of the journal is available online here: http://josephsmithpapers.org/paperSummary/history-1834- 1836?p=83&highlight=Letter%20VII

The book contained many blank pages. In 1839, the book was turned over to start the first volume of Joseph Smith's multivolume manuscript history. This is the history that the *Times and Seasons* began publishing on 15 March 1842, from which Joseph Smith—History was extracted.

Historians believe Joseph Smith "maintained custody of the volume through his later life."[12]

Re-publication

Oliver's description of Cumorah in New York was universally accepted by early Mormons, but the *Messenger and Advocate* had been published in 1835 and few people had access to Joseph's History 1834-1836.

In the ensuing years, many people joined the Church who had never read the *Messenger and Advocate*. President Cowdery's letters, including Letter VII, were republished several times during Joseph's lifetime, making them as widely available as possible.

1840—The Millennial Star.

The first reprinting of the letters appears to have been in the *Millennial Star*, a newspaper published in Manchester, England, by Parley P. Pratt beginning in May 1840. The June 1840 issue contains an article titled "A Remarkable Vision" that consists of portions of Letter IV. Pratt introduced the letter with this observation:

The following is an extract from the February number of the Latter-Day Saints Messenger and Advocate, published in Ohio,

---

[12] *Ibid*, Source Note, p. 25.

North America, 1835, being an extract of a letter written by Elder Oliver Cowdery, giving an account of the ministering of an ANGEL to Mr. Joseph Smith, jun.[13]

President Cowdery's letters were republished despite his having left the Church in 1838. Perhaps Pratt sought and obtained Joseph's permission first, although we do not have direct evidence of this if he did.

Joseph did give express permission to Benjamin Winchester some time in 1840 (see the section *1841—Gospel Reflector* below). Winchester may have communicated this to the Pratt brothers, or the Pratt brothers could have been part of the same conversation.

Winchester and the Pratt brothers worked closely together in 1839 and 1840. Winchester preached with Orson Pratt in New Jersey and attended a gathering at Parley's home in New York on 18 November 1839. Joseph Smith arrived in Philadelphia in December 1839 and stayed at Winchester's home through January 1840. Orson Pratt arrived in Philadelphia on December 21st and Parley arrived a few days later. On January 13, 1840, Joseph gave a sermon in Philadelphia that Parley described in his *Autobiography*.

Winchester and his wife visited England in August 1840 for six weeks, arriving after Letter IV was republished.

Additional extracts from President Cowdery's letters, each titled "A Remarkable Vision," were published in the *Millennial Star* as follows:

- September 1840 Letter VI (all but the first three introductory paragraphs and the last two paragraphs)

- October 1840: Letter VII (all but the first five introductory paragraphs)

---

[13] http://contentdm.lib.byu.edu/cdm/ref/collection/MStar/id/150

- November 1840: Letter VIII (all but the last eight paragraphs)
Letter I was published in full in January 1843, accompanied with a promise to publish all of the letters in a pamphlet. (See 1844– *Letters of Oliver Cowdery to W.W. Phelps* below)

1840—*Interesting Account.*

Orson Pratt included extracts and paraphrasing from Letters IV, VII and VIII in his influential pamphlet, *A[n] Interesting Account of Several Remarkable Visions*, published in Edinburgh in September 1840.[14] (The term "interesting account" comes from Letter I.) The Joseph Smith papers explain the significance of Pratt's work.

> Pratt's *Interesting Account of Several Remarkable Visions* proved to be one of the more influential Mormon tracts to come out of this period. The first American edition was printed in New York in 1841, and reprints appeared in Europe, Australia, and the United States. Pratt's work was a principal source for Orson Hyde's German-language pamphlet Ein Ruf aus der Wüste [A cry out of the wilderness], the earliest church publication in a language other than English, and for the first French-language pamphlet, John Taylor's Aux amis de la vérité religieuse [To friends of religious truth]. Pratt's pamphlet was later translated into Danish, Swedish, and Dutch.
>
> *Interesting Account* is not a JS document, because JS did not write it, assign it, or supervise its creation. However, two JS documents in this volume, "Church History" and "Latter Day Saints" (a later version of "Church History"), quote extensively from Pratt's pamphlet. These documents made use of Pratt's language to describe JS's early visionary experiences and built on Pratt's summary of the

---

[14] Because of its influence on the Wentworth Letter, the pamphlet is reproduced in the Joseph Smith Papers here: http://www.josephsmithpapers.org/paper-summary/appendix-orson-pratt-an-interesting-account-of-several-remarkable-visions-1840/1#full-transcript.

church's "faith and doctrine" for the thirteen-point statement of church beliefs that came to be known as the Articles of Faith.[15]

The document titled "Church History" is commonly known as the Wentworth Letter. It was published in the *Times and Seasons* on March 1, 1842. The Articles of Faith that don't have corresponding statements in Pratt's pamphlet (6, 9, 10, 11 & 13) appear to be adapted from Oliver's "we believe" statements in the October 1834 *Messenger and Advocate* that also contained Letter I.

The Wentworth Letter includes other wording that draws from Oliver's letters.

1841—*Times and Seasons.*

Don Carlos Smith, Joseph's younger brother, edited the *Times and Seasons* from its inception in 1839 through his death in September 1841. He had learned the newspaper and printing business in Kirtland, where he worked on the *Messenger and Advocate* and the *Elder's Journal.*

In the October 1840 edition of the *Times and Seasons*, Don Carlos observed that "we have an abundance of matter for the instruction of the saints, as President Joseph Smith jr. is furnishing us with essays on the glorious subject of the priesthood."[16] The next month, Don Carlos published Letter I below the heading "Copy of a Letter written by O. Cowdery, on the restoration of the

---

[15] Appendix: Orson Pratt, *A[n] Interesting Account of Several Remarkable Visions, 1840,* in History, 1834-1836, *The Joseph Smith Papers, Histories, Volume 1: Joseph Smith Histories, 1832-1844,* pp. 517-546. It is available online here: http://josephsmithpapers.org/paperSummary/appendix-orson-pratt-an-interesting-account-of-several-remarkable-visions-1840

[16] *Times and Seasons*, 1:12 (Oct. 1840), p. 192.

Priesthood." The only references to the Priesthood in this issue are found in President Cowdery's letter, suggesting that the essays Joseph furnished to his brother were actually the eight letters.

When Don Carlos began serializing the letters in the *Times and Seasons*, he introduced them this way:

> As the greater portion of our readers, are those who have not had the priviledge [privilege] of being conversant with the former publications of this church, we therefore, deem it proper to extract some articles from them. We have commenced, in this number a series of letters written by O. Cowdery, in 1834, on the subject of the coming forth of the Book of Mormon, the rise of the church, and the restoration of the Priesthood; these three subjects excite more curiosity, create more enquiry [inquiry], and cause more labor to answer, than any others of our faith. Therefore, that all who wish, may have the desired intelligence, we shall publish them from the pen of a living witness. (emphasis added) *Times and Seasons*, Vol. 1. No. 1., November 1, 1840 [Whole No. 13]

Don Carlos published the seven subsequent letters under the title "Rise of the Church," appearing as the first articles in four subsequent issues of the *Times and Seasons* (Nov.15, Dec. 1, Dec. 15, and May 1). In April, the letters were published in the interior of the newspaper. The title was printed in all caps in all but the final installment.

Nov. 15, 1840: RISE OF THE CHURCH LETTER II
Dec. 1, 1840: RISE OF THE CHURCH LETTER III
Dec. 15, 1840: RISE OF THE CHURCH LETTER IV
Apr. 1, 1841, p. 360: RISE OF THE CHURCH LETTER VI
(Note: the last two paragraphs of Letter VI and the first two paragraphs of Letter VII were omitted, so this article flows from

Letter VI into Letter VII without designating the beginning of Letter VII)

April 15, 1841, p. 377: RISE OF THE CHURCH (Note: this article is a continuation of Letter VII, beginning with "Alternately, as we could naturally expect…")

May 1, 1841, p. 391: Rise of the Church [Concluded.] Letter VIII

Don Carlos made editorial changes to the letters, such as omitting references to Phelps and the changes noted above. Other reprintings, including Winchester's, also omitted the original references to Phelps. It is unknown whether Don Carlos had original copies of the letters or if he copied them from the *Messenger and Advocate,* but he did avoid minor copy errors that appear in Joseph's journal.

The Cumorah portion of Letter VII was published on 15 April 1841 (*Times and Seasons,* Vol 2, No. 12, p. 377).

1841—*Gospel Reflector.*

Benjamin Winchester published all of Cowdery's letters in the March 15, 1841, edition of his Philadelphia newspaper titled the *Gospel Reflector.*[17] In his first issue, 1 January 1841, Winchester made it clear to his readers that before publishing his newspaper, he

---

[17] The *Gospel Reflector* was originally issued in single issues on the 1st and 15th of each month, like the *Times and Seasons.* It was published for six months. Bound copies of the twelve issues were sold in Nauvoo. A bound reproduction was produced by Richard Drew, Burlington [Voree], Wisconsin in 1993. *Gospel Reflector* is available online from several sources, including this one: https://archive.org/details/gospelreflectori00winc

had sought and obtained approval from church leaders, including Joseph Smith and Sidney Rigdon.[18]

> I would here observe to the members of the church in this section of country, that I had it (as is well known) in contemplation last spring to publish O. Cowdery's letters giving a history of the coming forth of The Book of Mormon and, connected, with them, other original matter, such as I had written myself, **which I asked permission or advice of J. Smith who said I was at liberty to publish any thing of the kind that would further the cause of righteousness.** I also asked advice of S. Rigdon, who said he had no objection.

Perhaps Winchester felt obligated to obtain this approval because Oliver had left the Church and was no longer affiliated with it. That Joseph and President Rigdon nevertheless endorsed the letters is another affirmation of their legitimacy.

Winchester published his own commentary on the Book of Mormon in the 1 and 15 March 1841 issues of the *Gospel Reflector*. He added Oliver's letters at the end of the 15 March issue, introducing them with this:

> The following Letters of Oliver Cowdery were first published in the "Messenger and Advocate," in Kirtland, Ohio, A. D. 1834-5. Believing they will be read with great interest, and satisfactorily received by all our patrons; therefore, we cheerfully insert them in the "Gospel Reflector."* Indeed, the particularities, and important

---

[18] On 14 May 1840, Joseph Smith wrote a letter to Orson Hyde and John E. Page, telling them that "With respect to publishing any other work, either original, or those which have been published before, you will be governed by circumstances; if you think necessary to do so I shall have no objections whatever." JS, Letter, Nauvoo, IL, to Orson Hyde and John E. Page, Cincinnati, OH; in JS Letterbook 2, pp. 146–147.

incidents, connected with the coming forth of the Book of Mormon, have ever been, and are now, a subject of inquiry. The following Letters contain all the information necessary upon that subject.

*N. B. They were written to W. W. Phelps, who wrote answers to them ; but we shall not publish them : for he was also a member of the society ; and his letters were generally brief — questions upon the above subject. This will account for the style in which the following are written.

Winchester edited the letters. In addition to omitting references to Phelps, he deleted the first five paragraphs of Letter VII, apparently because those introductory paragraphs are rhetorical instead of historical. Winchester also included the letter written by Joseph Smith that is included in Appendix II of this book, which Oliver published in December 1834. Winchester also changed the spelling in the letters to conform to British conventions.

1842 – D&C 128.

Section 128 is "An epistle from Joseph Smith the Prophet to The Church of Jesus Christ of Latter-day Saints, containing further directions on baptism for the dead, dated at Nauvoo, Illinois, September 6, 1842."[19] However, two verses summarize significant events in the restoration that correspond to many of the events Oliver addressed in the historical letters. Readers of the *Times and Seasons* were already familiar with the letters and would understand the context of Joseph's epistle accordingly.

---

[19] Introduction to Section 128. https://www.lds.org/scriptures/dc-testament/dc/128?lang=eng.

The following verse-by-verse commentary suggests how Joseph's contemporaries would have understood his references.

20 And again, what do we hear? Glad tidings from Cumorah!
[In Letter VII, Oliver wrote in detail about Cumorah, correcting the spelling in the 1830 edition of the Book of Mormon and explaining that Mormon's depository of records was inside the same hill in New York where Joseph found the plates. Oliver also stated it was a fact that the final battles of the Jaredites and the Nephites took place in the mile-wide valley west of the Hill Cumorah and explained that only thousands of Jaredites and tens of thousands of Nephites and Lamanites died there, an important clarification of the text that has long been overlooked.]

Moroni, an angel from heaven, declaring the fulfilment of the prophets—the book to be revealed.
[In Letters IV, V and VI, Oliver described Moroni's visit in detail and explained how the prophecies in the Old Testament were being fulfilled.]

A voice of the Lord in the wilderness of Fayette, Seneca county, declaring the three witnesses to bear record of the book!
[Oliver was one of the Three Witnesses and likely composed their testimony. He also possessed the printer's manuscript and Joseph's seer stone.]

The voice of Michael on the banks of the Susquehanna, detecting the devil when he appeared as an angel of light!
[Nothing more is known of this incident, but because Oliver spent time with Joseph along the Susquehanna, it seems likely he

was involved. Perhaps the experience related to the Book of Moses in some way. Oliver acted as scribe for much of that book.]

The voice of Peter, James, and John in the wilderness between Harmony, Susquehanna county, and Colesville, Broome county, on the Susquehanna river, declaring themselves as possessing the keys of the kingdom, and of the dispensation of the fulness of times!

[Oliver accompanied Joseph when they received the Priesthood keys from Peter, James and John. Apparently this was a progressive restoration of keys.]

21 And again, the voice of God in the chamber of old Father Whitmer, in Fayette, Seneca county,

[This could be an allusion to the translation of the Fayette plates in the upper chamber of Father Whitmer's house.]

and at sundry times, and in divers places through all the travels and tribulations of this Church of Jesus Christ of Latter-day Saints! And the voice of Michael, the archangel; the voice of Gabriel, and of Raphael, and of divers angels, from Michael or Adam down to the present time, all declaring their dispensation, their rights, their keys, their honors, their majesty and glory, and the power of their priesthood; giving line upon line, precept upon precept; here a little, and there a little; giving us consolation by holding forth that which is to come, confirming our hope!

[Oliver and Joseph, together, received the Priesthood keys in the Kirtland temple from Moses, Elijah, Elias, and the Lord Himself, as described in D&C 110.]

1844 – *Letters of Oliver Cowdery to W. W. Phelps.*
An anonymous pamphlet containing all the letters was published in Liverpool in 1844.[20]

The Preface to the pamphlet gives a sense of how much these letters were in demand.

> **We have frequently been solicited to publish**, in pamphlet form, the following letters of OLIVER COWDERY, addressed to W. W. PHELPS. We at last avail ourselves of the opportunity to do so, being fully assured that they will be read with great interest by the Saints generally; while from the peculiar work on which they treat, together with the spirit of truthfulness in which they are written, not forgetting their style as compositions, we have no doubt but that many of the honest-hearted may, by their perusal, be led to a further examination of those principles, the origin of which is therein set forth.

There are variations in punctuation and spelling that indicate the pamphlet was copied from Winchester's version. For example, the *Messenger and Advocate*, the *Times and Seasons*, and Joseph's journal all use the term "enquirers" in Letter II. Winchester changed it to "inquirers," and the 1844 pamphlet also uses "inquirers." Winchester changed the original "opponants" to "opponents," as it also appears in the 1844 pamphlet. Winchester changed the original spelling "Savior" and "favor" to "Saviour" and "favour" as the terms are also spelled in the pamphlet. The letter from Joseph Smith to Cowdery at the end of the pamphlet uses the Winchester spelling as well.

---

[20] The pamphlet is available online at https://archive.org/details/lettersbyoliverc00oliv

In the pamphlet, Letter VII begins with the sixth paragraph like Winchester's version. Winchester wrote the "N.B." quoted above to explain Phelps' connection, while the pamphlet says: "It will be understood that Brother PHELPS wrote answers to these letters, which generally contained some questions upon the subject treated of, accounting for the style in which they are written."

The editor (or typesetter) in Liverpool made a few changes to Winchester's version. In some cases Winchester retains spelling from the original, such as "snears of bigots," that the 1844 pamphlet changes, in this case to "sneers of bigots." In other places, Winchester retained the original punctuation while the pamphlet has some differences.

1844—The Prophet.

Oliver's letters were published serially in the Mormon newspaper titled *The Prophet* in New York City starting with the inaugural issue in May 1844. William Smith became the editor of the paper as of the June 29th issue—two days after the martyrdom.

That issue contained Letter VII.

1851 through the present—Pearl of Great Price.

Joseph Smith—History 1:71 features an asterisk that corresponds to an excerpt from Letter I about the appearance of John the Baptist. (The Pearl of Great Price was officially canonized in general conference on October 10, 1880).

In light of the frequent republication of President Cowdery's letters, it is not surprising that when he collected the materials for the Pearl of Great Price in 1851, Franklin D. Richards included this portion of Letter I. The eight letters were well-known in England at the time, thousands of copies having been published in 1844.

The current edition of the Pearl of Great Price cites the *Messenger and Advocate*, vol. 1 (October 1834), pp. 14-16. Because few living Church members recognize the *Messenger and Advocate*, I think it would be a good idea to change the reference in the Pearl of Great Price to *History*, 1834-1836 in the Joseph Smith papers.

1899—The Improvement Era.

The letters were again reprinted in the *Improvement Era* in a series titled "Early Scenes and Incidents in the Church." The July 1899 issue[21] contains Letter VII. In 1899, Joseph F. Smith was the Editor of the *Improvement Era*. He was also Second Counselor in the First Presidency under President Wilford Woodruff. He had been an Apostle for 33 years by that point, and had served as a counselor in the First Presidency under both Brigham Young and John Taylor.

These multiple republications of Letter VII, including the copy written into Joseph Smith's personal journal, demonstrate how important Letter VII was to the early leaders of the Church—particularly Joseph Smith. Although there was speculation about various Book of Mormon sites such as Zarahemla and Lehi's landing site, there was universal agreement that Cumorah was in New York, just as Letter VII said.

--->>> <<<---

Acceptance of the New York setting for Cumorah persisted after Joseph's death. In 1879, Orson Pratt divided the text of the Book of Mormon into chapters and verses. He also added footnotes, some

---

[21] Online at https://archive.org/stream/improvementera29unse#page/652/mode/2up.

of which suggested locations of Book of Mormon sites, such as note *k* to 1 Nephi 19:23, "**Believed to be** on the coast of Chile, S. America," and note *g* to Omni 1:12, "The land Nephi is **supposed to have been** in or near Ecuador, South America."

But when it came to the location of Cumorah, Pratt's footnotes were not speculative or equivocal. Note *a* to Mormon 6:2 declares, "The hill Cumorah is in Manchester, Ontario Co., N. York."

Pratt's footnotes were removed in 1920, but they help demonstrate that for the first 90 years of Church history, there was no doubt that Cumorah was in New York.

President Cowdery's letters, ubiquitous during Joseph's lifetime, have largely faded into oblivion.

So far as I've been able to determine, apart for the footnote from Joseph Smith—History, Oliver's historical letters have never been published in the *Ensign* or in any Church lesson manuals.[22]

Nevertheless, apostles and prophets have affirmed the New York location of Cumorah several times in General Conference and in their other writings.

For example, in his book *Articles of Faith*, Elder James E. Talmage of the Quorum of the Twelve wrote:

> The final struggles between Nephites and Lamanites were waged **in the vicinity of the Hill Cumorah, in what is now the State of New York**, resulting in the destruction of the Nephites as a nation, about 400 A.D. The last Nephite representative was Moroni, who, wandering for safety from place to place, daily

---

[22] Letter VII begins on page 72 of *Histories, Volume 1, Joseph Smith Histories*, 1832-1844, Joseph Smith Papers (The Church Historian's Press, 2012). You can find it online by going to www.josephsmithpapers.org and searching for "Letter VII."

expecting death from the victorious Lamanites, wrote the concluding parts of the Book of Mormon, and hid the record in Cumorah.

Elder LeGrand Richards of the Quorum of the Twelve wrote this in *A Marvelous Work and a Wonder*:

> It was at this time that Mormon deposited in the Hill Cumorah all the records that had been entrusted to him except a few plates that he gave to his son Moroni. (See Mormon 6.)
> About A.D. 420, Moroni placed these plates with those his father, Mormon, had already deposited in the hill. (See Moroni 10:1-2.)

No prophet or apostle has publicly specified a location for Cumorah *other* than in New York.

Consequently, the "two-Cumorahs theory" is purely a creation of intellectuals. Any theory or model of Book of Mormon geography that puts Cumorah anywhere other than in New York constitutes a repudiation of the prophets and apostles, starting with Joseph and Oliver.

Chapter 5 – Cumorah in Letter VII

Although all the letters are important, Letter VII is especially significant because of the role it plays in describing the only specific modern location of a known Book of Mormon site—the Hill Cumorah.

Oliver, who noted at the outset that his letters were written with the assistance of Joseph Smith and would be "founded upon facts," unequivocally describes the New York Cumorah as the scene of the last battles of the Jaredites and the Nephites and the location of Mormon's depository of Nephite records.

This chapter excerpts the Cumorah material directly from the *Messenger and Advocate*, July 1835 and October 1835 (for letter VIII). All emphasis is added.

As you read the extracts, notice how specific and detailed President Cowdery's account is. Remember that he is responding to anti-Mormon claims that the Book of Mormon was not an actual history.

One often overlooked aspect of Letter VII is Oliver's explanation of the number of people who died at Cumorah. Some readers have assumed that millions of Jaredites died there, but President Cowdery explains it was only a few thousand. His accounting makes sense when we read Ether 13 carefully and recognize that the final battle lasted only a week. After six days, there were only 121 people left. The next day, there were only 59 left. Even if we assume that half the people were killed each day, doubling it backward calculates to about 7,744 on the first day of battle.

Letter VII also indicates that only tens of thousands of Nephites and Lamanites died at Cumorah—far fewer than many people have assumed. But again, President Cowdery's explanation fits the narrative. When we read Mormon 6:11-12 carefully, we realize he could see only 20,000 people from the top of the Hill Cumorah. The other groups of ten thousand Mormon lists had died previously in the wars, far from Cumorah.[23]

Cumorah extract from Letter VII

LETTER VII.

I must now give you some description of the place where, and the manner in which these records were deposited.

You are acquainted with the mail road from Palmyra, Wayne Co. to Canandaigua, Ontario Co. N. Y.[24] and also, as you pass from the former to the latter place, before arriving at the little village of Manchester, say from three to four, or about four miles from Palmyra, you pass a large hill on the east side of the road. Why I say large, is, because it is as large perhaps, as any in that country. To a person acquainted with this road, a description would be unnecessary, as **it is the largest and rises the highest of any on that route.** The north end rises quite sudden until it assumes a level with the more southerly extremity, and I think I may say an elevation higher than at the south a short distance, say half or three fourths of a mile. As you pass toward Canandaigua it lessens gradually

---

[23] For my analysis of this point, see my blog post here: http://www.lettervii.com/2017/07/more-about-cumorahs-casualties.html

[24] Phelps was familiar with Canandaigua because he lived there from 1827-8 and published and edited the Ontario Phoenix there.

until the surface assumes its common level, or is broken by other smaller hills or ridges, water courses and ravines. I think I am justified in saying that this is the highest hill for some distance round, and I am certain that its appearance, as it rises so suddenly from a plain on the north, must attract the notice of the traveller as he passes by.

At about one mile west rises another ridge of less height, running parallel with the former, leaving a beautiful vale between. The soil is of the first quality for the country, and under a state of cultivation, which gives a prospect at once imposing, when one reflects on the fact, that here, between these hills, the entire power and national strength of both the Jaredites and Nephites were destroyed.

By turning to the 529th and 530th pages of the Book of Mormon, you will read Mormon's account of the last great struggle of his people, as they were encamped round this hill Cumorah. (It is printed Camorah, which is an error.) In this valley fell the remaining strength and pride of a once powerful people, the Nephites—once so highly favored of the Lord, but at that time in darkness, doomed to suffer extermination by the hand of their barbarous and uncivilized brethren. From the top of this hill, Mormon, with a few others, after the battle, gazed with horror upon the mangled remains of those who, the day before, were filled with anxiety, hope, or doubt. A few had fled to the South, who were hunted down by the victorious party, and all who would not deny the Savior and his religion, were put to death. Mormon himself, according to the record of his son Moroni, was also slain.

But a long time previous to this national disaster it appears from his own account, he foresaw approaching destruction. In fact, if he perused the records of his fathers, which were in his possession, he could have learned that such would be the case. Alma, who lived before the coming of the Messiah, prophesies this. He however, by Divine appointment, abridged from those records, in his own style and language, a short account of the more important and prominent items, from the days of Lehi to his own time, after which **he deposited, as he says, on the 529th page, all the records in this same hill, Cumorah,** and after gave his small record to his son Moroni, who, as appears from the same, finished it, after witnessing the extinction of his people as a nation.

It was not the wicked who overcame the righteous: far from this: it was the wicked against the wicked, and by the wicked the wicked were punished. The Nephites who were once enlightened, had fallen from a more elevated standing as to favour and privilege before the Lord, in consequence of the righteousness of their fathers, and now falling below, for such was actually the case, were suffered to be overcome, and the land was left to the possession of the red men, who were without intelligence, only in the affairs of their wars; and **having no records, only preserving their history by tradition from father to son, lost the account of their true origin, and wandered from river to river, from hill to hill, from mountain to mountain, and from sea to sea,** till the land was again peopled, in a measure, by a rude, wild, revengeful, warlike and barbarous race. Such are our Indians.

This hill, by the Jaredites, was called Ramah: by it, or around it, pitched the famous army of Coriantumr their tent. Coriantumr was the last king of the Jaredites. **The opposing army were to the west, and in this same valley, and near by. From day to day, did that mighty race spill their blood, in wrath, contending as it were, brother against brother, and father against son. In this same spot, in full view from the top of this same hill, one may gaze with astonishment upon the ground which was twice covered with the dead and dying of our fellowmen.**

Here may be seen, where once sunk to nought the pride and strength of two mighty nations; and here may be contemplated in solitude, while nothing but the faithful record of Mormon and Moroni is now extant to inform us of the fact, scenes of misery and distress—the aged, whose silver locks in other places, and at other times, would command reverence; the mother, who, in other circumstances would be spared from violence— the infant, whose tender cries would be regarded and listened to with a feeling of compassion and tenderness— and the virgin, whose grace, beauty and modesty, would be esteemed and held inviolate by all good men and enlightened and civilized nations, were alike disregarded and treated with scorn! In vain did the hoary head and man of gray hairs ask for mercy—in vain did the mother plead for compassion—in vain did the helpless and harmless infant weep for very anguish—and in vain did the virgin seek to escape the ruthless hand of revengeful foes and demons in human form—all alike were trampled down by the feet of the strong, and crushed beneath the rage of battle and war! Alas! who can reflect upon the last struggles of great and populous nations, sinking to dust beneath the hand of justice and retribution, without weeping over the corruption of the human heart, and sighing for the hour when the clangor of arms shall no more be heard, nor the calamities of contending armies be any more experienced for a thousand years? Alas! the calamity of war, the extinction of nations, the ruin of kingdoms, the fall of empires, and the dissolution of governments! Oh! the misery, distress and evil attendant, on these. Who can contemplate like scenes without sorrowing, and who so destitute of commiseration as not to be pained that man has fallen so low, so far beneath the station in which he was created?

In this vale lie commingled, in one mass of ruin, the ashes of thousands, and in this vale were destined to be consumed the fair forms and vigorous systems of tens of thousands of the human race—blood mixed with blood, flesh with flesh, bones with bones, and dust with dust! When the vital spark which animated their clay had fled, each lifeless lump lay on one common level—cold and inanimate. Those bosoms which had burned with rage against each other for real or supposed injury, had now ceased to heave with malice; those arms which were a few moments before nerved with strength, had alike become paralyzed, and those hearts which had been fired with revenge, had now ceased to beat, and the head to think—in silence, in solitude, and in disgrace alike, they have long since turned to earth, to their mother dust, to await the august, and to millions, awful hour, when the trump of the Son of God shall echo and re-echo from the skies, and they come forth quickened and immortalized, to not only stand in each other's presence, but before the bar of him who is Eternal!

With sentiments of pure respect, I conclude by subscribing myself your brother in the gospel.

-->>> <<<--

In Letter VIII, President Cowdery gives additional facts about the Hill Cumorah itself. Keep in mind that Oliver had personally visited Mormon's depository in the Hill Cumorah, had handled the plates, and had seen the other Nephite plates and artifacts.

Notice also how Oliver clearly delineates his speculation from fact; i.e., he doesn't know how deep Moroni originally buried the box, and he invites his readers to make up their own minds on that point. But he provides specific details about the size and contents of the box. Note also that it did not contain the sword of Laban or the Liahona, as some have claimed—and as some artwork depicts.

Cumorah extract from Letter VIII

LETTER VIII.

DEAR BROTHER,

IN my last I said I should give, partially, a "description of the place where, and the manner in which these records were deposited:" the first promise I have fulfilled, and must proceed to the latter:

The hill of which I have been speaking, at the time mentioned, presented a varied appearance: the north end rose suddenly from the plain, forming a promontory without timber, but covered with grass. As you passed to the south you soon came to scattering timber, the surface having been cleared by art or by wind; and a short distance further left, you are surrounded with the common forest of the country.

It is necessary to observe, that even the part cleared was only occupied for pasturage, its steep ascent and narrow summit not admitting the plow of the husbandman with any degree of ease or profit. It was at the second mentioned place where the record was found to be deposited, on the west side of the hill, not far from the top down its side; and **when myself visited the place in the year 1830, there were several trees standing: enow [enough] to cause a shade in summer, but not so much as to prevent the surface being covered with grass—which was also the case when the record was first found.**

Whatever may be the feeling of men on the reflection of past acts which have been performed on certain portions or spots of this earth, I know not, neither does it add or diminish to nor from the reality of my subject. When Moses heard the voice of God, at the foot of Horeb, out of the burning bush, he was commanded to take his shoes off his feet, for the ground on which he stood was holy. The same may be observed when Joshua beheld the "Captain of the Lord's host" by Jerico. And I confess that my mind was filled with many reflections; and though I did not *then* loose my shoe, yet with gratitude to God did I offer up the sacrifice of my heart.

How far below the surface these records were placed by Moroni, I am unable to say; but from the fact that they had been some fourteen hundred years buried, and that too on the side of a hill so steep, one is ready to conclude that they were some feet below, as the

earth would naturally wear more or less in that length of time. But they being placed toward the top of the hill, the ground would not remove as much as two-thirds, perhaps.

Another circumstance would prevent a wearing of the earth: in all probability, as soon as timber had time to grow, the hill was covered, after the Nephites were destroyed, and the roots of the same would hold the surface. However, on this point I shall leave every man to draw his own conclusion and form his own speculation, as I only promised to give a description of the place at the time the records were found in 1823.

It is sufficient for my present purpose, to know that such is the fact, that in 1823, yes, 1823, a man with whom I have had the most intimate and personal acquaintance, for almost seven years, actually discovered by the vision of God, the plates from which the Book of Mormon, as much as it is disbelieved, was translated! Such is the case, though men rack their very brains to invent falsehoods, and then waft them upon every breeze, to the contrary notwithstanding.

I have now given sufficient on the subject of the hill Cumorah—it has a singular and imposing appearance for that country, and must excite the curious enquiry of every lover of the Book of Mormon, though, I hope, never like Jerusalem and the sepulchre of our Lord, the pilgrims. In my estimation, certain places are dearer to me for what they *now* contain, than for what they *have* contained. For the satisfaction of such as believed I have been thus particular, and to avoid the question being a thousand times asked, more than any other cause, shall proceed and be as particular as heretofore.

The manner in which the plates were deposited.

First, a hole of sufficient depth, (how deep I know not,) was dug. At the bottom of this was laid a stone of suitable size, the upper surface being smooth. At each edge was placed a large quantity of cement, and into this cement, at the four edges of this stone were placed erect, four others, *their* bottom edges resting *in* the cement at the outer edges of the first stone. The four last named, when placed erect, formed a box, the corners, or where the edges of the four came in contact, were also cemented so firmly that the moisture from without was prevented from entering.

It is to be observed, also, that the inner surface of the four erect, or side stones was smooth. This box was sufficiently large to admit a breast-plate, such as was used by the ancients to defend the chest, &c., from the arrows and weapons of their enemy. From the bottom of the box, or from the breast-plate, arose three small pillars composed of the same description of cement used on the edges; and upon these three pillars was placed the record of the children of Joseph, and of a people who left the tower far, far before the days of Joseph, or a sketch of each, which had it not been for this, and the never failing goodness of God, *we* might have perished in our sins, having been left to bow down before the altars of the Gentiles, and to have paid homage to the priests of Baal!

I must not forget to say that this box, containing the record was covered with another stone, the bottom surface being flat and the upper, crowning. But those three pillars were not so lengthy as to cause the plates and the crowning stone to come in contact. I have now given you, according to my promise, the manner in which this record was deposited; though when it was first visited by our brother, in 1823, a part of the crowning stone was visible above the surface, while the edges were concealed by the soil and grass, from which circumstance you will see, that however deep this box might have been placed by Moroni at first, the time had been sufficient to wear the earth so that it was easily discovered, when once directed, and yet not enough to make a *perceivable* difference to the passer by.

So wonderful are the works of the Almighty, and so far from our finding out are his ways, that one who trembles to take his holy name into his lips, is left to wonder at his exact providences, and the fulfilment of his purposes in the event of times and seasons. **A few years sooner might have found even the top stone concealed, and discouraged our brother from attempting to make a further trial to obtain this rich treasure, for fear of discovery; and a few later might have left the small box uncovered, and exposed its valuable contents to the rude calculations and vain speculations of those who neither understand common language nor fear God.**

But such would have been contrary to the words of the ancients and the promises made to them; and this is why I am left to admire the works and see the wisdom in the designs of the Lord in all things manifested to the eyes of the world: they show that all human inventions are like the vapors, while his word endures forever and his promises to the last generation.

Chapter 6 – Letter I

October 1834, *Messenger and Advocate*

Oliver's letters provide numerous details that help modern-day readers form a better mental picture of the early events in Church history. Throughout, he emphasizes he is relating facts.

I have edited the letters to focus on the key points that make them so useful today. I have also added emphasis.

In Letter I, Oliver describes the restoration of the Aaronic Priesthood, an account included in the Pearl of Great Price as a note at the end of Joseph Smith-History.

Norton, Medina County, Ohio
Sabbath Evening, September 7, 1834.

DEAR BROTHER, BEFORE leaving home I promised if I tarried long to write and while a few moments are now allowed me for reflection aside from the cares and common conversation of my friends in this place I have thought that were I to communicate them to you, you might, perhaps, if they should not prove *especially* beneficial to yourself, by confirming you in the faith of the gospel, at least be interesting, since it has pleased our heavenly Father to call us both to rejoice in the same hope of eternal life. **And by giving them publicity some thousands who have embraced the same covenant, may learn something more particular upon the rise of this church in this last time.** And while the grey evening is fast changing into a settled darkness, my heart responds with the happy millions who are in the presence of the Lamb, and are past the power of temptation in rendering thanks, though feebly, to the same parent.

Another day has passed into that, to us boundless ocean, ETERNITY! where nearly six thousand years have gone before; and what flits across the mind like an electric shock is, that it will never return! Whether it has been well improved or not; whether the principles emanating from HIM who "hallowed" it have been observed; or whether, like the common mass of time, it has been heedlessly spent, is not for me to say—one thing I can say—it can never be recalled! it has rolled in to assist in filling up the grand space decreed in the mind of its Author, till nature shall have ceased her work, and *time* its accustomed revolutions—when its Lord shall have completed the gathering of his elect, and with them enjoy that Sabbath which shall never end!

On Friday, the 5th, in company with our brother JOSEPH SMITH jun., I left Kirtland for this place (New Portage,) to attend the conference previously appointed. To be permitted once more to travel with this brother, occasions reflections of no ordinary kind. **Many have been the fatigues and privations which have fallen to my lot to endure for the gospel's sake, since 1828, with this brother.** Our road has frequently been spread with the "fowler's snare," and our persons sought with the eagerness of the Savage's ferocity for innocent blood, by men either heated to desperation by the insinuations of those who professed to be "guides and way-marks" to the kingdom of glory, or the individuals themselves! **This, I confess, is a dark picture to spread before our patrons, but they will pardon my plainness when I assure them of the truth.** In fact, God has so ordered, that the reflections which I am permitted to cast upon my past life, relative to a knowledge of the way of salvation, are rendered "doubly endearing."

Not only have I been graciously preserved from wicked and unreasonable men, with this our brother, but I have seen the fruit of

perseverance in proclaiming the everlasting gospel, immediately after it was declared to the world in these last days, in a manner not to be forgotten while heaven gives me common intellect. And what serves to render the reflection past expression on this point is, that from *his* hand I received baptism, by the direction of the angel of God— the first received into this church in this day.

Near this time of the setting of the sun, Sabbath evening, April 5th, 1829, my natural eyes for the first time beheld this brother: he then resided in Harmony, Susquehanna county Penn. On Monday, the 6th, I assisted him in arranging some business of a temporal nature, and on Tuesday, the 7th, commenced to write the Book of Mormon.

These were days never to be forgotten; to sit under the sound of a voice dictated by the *inspiration* of heaven, awakened the utmost gratitude of this bosom! Day after day I continued, uninterrupted, to write from his mouth, as he translated with the *Urim* and *Thummim,* or, as the Nephites would have said, "interpreters," the history or record called "The Book of Mormon."

To notice, in even few words, the interesting account given by Mormon and his faithful son Moroni, of a people once beloved and favored of heaven, would supersede my present design; I shall therefore defer this to a future period, and, as I said in the introduction, pass more directly to some few incidents immediately connected with the rise of this church, which may be entertaining to some thousands who have stepped forward, amid the frowns of bigots and the calumny of hypocrites, and embraced the gospel of Christ. No men in their sober senses could translate and write the directions given to the Nephites, from the mouth of the Savior of the precise manner in which men should build up his church and especially when corruption had spread an uncertainty over all forms and systems practised among men, without desiring a privilege of showing the willingness of the heart by being buried in the liquid grave, to answer a "good conscience by the resurrection of Jesus Christ."

After writing the account given of the Saviour's ministry to the remnant of the seed of Jacob upon this continent, it was easily to be seen, as the prophet said would be, that darkness covered the earth and, gross darkness the minds of the people. On reflecting further, it was as easily to be seen, that amid the great strife and noise concerning religion, none had authority from God to administer the ordinances of the gospel. For, the question might be asked, have men authority to administer in the name of Christ who deny revelations, when *his* testimony is no less than the spirit of prophecy, and his religion based, built, and sustained by immediate revelations in all ages of the world when he has had a people on earth? If these facts were buried and carefully concealed by men whose craft would have been in danger, if once permitted to shine in the faces of men, they were no longer to us, and we only waited for the commandment to be given, "Arise and be baptized."

This was not long desired before it was realized. The Lord, who is rich in mercy, and ever willing to answer the consistent prayer of the humble, after we had called upon him in a fervent manner, aside from the abodes of men, condescended to manifest to us his will. On a sudden, as from the midst of eternity, the voice of the Redeemer spake peace to us, while the vail was parted and the angel of God came down clothed with glory, and delivered the anxiously-looked-for message and the keys of the gospel of repentance. What joy! what wonder! what amazement! While the world were racked and distracted—while millions were groping as the blind for the wall, and while all men were resting upon uncertainty, as a general mass, our eyes beheld—our ears heard, as in the "blaze of day;" yes, more—above the glitter of the May sun-beam, which then shed its brilliancy over the face of nature! Then his voice, though mild, pierced to the centre, and his words "I am thy fellow-servant," dispelled every fear. We listened—we gazed—we admired! 'Twas the voice of the angel from glory—'twas a message from the Most High! and as we heard we rejoiced, while his love enkindled upon our souls, and we were wrapt in the vision of the Almighty! Where was room for doubt? No where; uncertainty had fled, doubt had sunk no more to rise, while fiction and deception had fled forever!

But, dear brother, think further, think for a moment what joy filled our hearts and with what surprise we must have bowed, (for who would not have bowed the knee for such a blessing?) when we received under his hand the holy priesthood, as he said, "upon you my fellow servants, in the name of Messiah I confer this priesthood and this authority, which shall remain upon earth, that the sons of Levi may yet offer an offering unto the Lord in righteousness!"

I shall not attempt to paint to you the feelings of this heart, nor the majestic beauty and glory which surrounded us on this occasion; but you will believe me when I say, that earth, nor men, with the eloquence of time, cannot begin to clothe language in as interesting and sublime a manner as this holy personage. No; nor has this earth power to give the joy, to bestow the peace, or comprehend the wisdom which was contained in each sentence as they were delivered by the power of the Holy Spirit! Man may deceive his fellow man— deception may follow deception, and the children of the wicked one may have power to seduce the foolish and untaught, till naught but fiction feeds the many, and the fruit of falsehood carries in its current the giddy to the grave; but one touch with the finger of his love, yes, one ray of glory from the upper world, or one word from the mouth of the Saviour, from the bosom of eternity, strikes it *all* into insignificance, and blots it forever from the mind! The assurance that we were in the presence of an angel—the certainty that we heard the voice of Jesus—and the truth unsullied as it flowed from a pure personage, dictated by the will of God, is to me past description, and I shall ever look upon this expression of the Saviour's goodness with wonder and thanksgiving while I am permitted to tarry, and in those mansions where perfection dwells and sin never comes, I hope to adore in that DAY which shall never cease!*

I must close for the present: my candle is quite extinguished, and all nature seems locked in silence, shrouded in darkness, and enjoying that repose so necessary to this life. But the period is rolling on when *night* will close, and those who are found worthy will inherit that city where neither the light of the sun nor moon will be necessary! "for the glory of God will lighten it, and the Lamb will be the light thereof."

*I will hereafter give you a full history of the rise of this church, up to the time stated in my introduction; which will necessarily embrace the life and character of this brother. I shall therefore leave the history of baptism, &c., till its proper place.

Chapter 7 – Letter II

November 1834, *Messenger and Advocate*

Letter II reviews how the world receives the prophets of God and explains that prophets are imperfect men. This is a counter-argument to the attacks on the character of Joseph and his family that were published in *Mormonism Unvailed* in October 1834.

LETTER II.

DEAR BROTHER, IN the last *Messenger and Advocate*, I promised to commence a more particular or minute history of the rise and progress of the church of the Latter-day Saints, and publish for the benefit of inquirers and all who are disposed to learn. There are certain facts relative to the works of God worthy the consideration and observance of every individual, and every society:—they are, that he never works in the dark—his works are always performed in a clear, intelligible manner; and another point is, that he never works in vain. This is not the case with men, but might it not be? When the Lord works, he accomplishes his purposes, and the effects of his power are to be seen afterward. In view of this, suffer me to make a few remarks by way of introduction.

[This introduction is omitted.]

I cannot reasonably expect, then, that the large majority of professors will be willing to listen to my argument for a moment, as a careful, impartial, and faithful investigation of the doctrines which I believe to be correct, and the principles cherished in my bosom and believed by this church, by every honest man, must be admitted as truth.

Of this I may say as Tertullian said to the Emperor when writing in defence [defense] of the saints in his day: "Whoever looked well into our religion that did not embrace it?"

...

Look at pure religion whenever it has had a place on earth, and you will always mark the same characteristics in all its features. Look at truth (without which the former could not exist), and the same peculiarities are apparent. Those who have been guided by them have always shown the same principles; and those who were not have as uniformly sought to destroy their influence. ...

Enoch walked with God, and was taken home without tasting death. Why were not *all* converted in his day and taken with him to glory? Noah, it is said, was perfect in his generation; and it is plain that he had communion with his Maker, and by HIS direction accomplished a work, the parallel of which is not to be found in the annals of the world! Why were not the *world* converted, that the flood might have been stayed? Men, from the days of our father Abraham, have talked, boasted, and extolled his faith: and he is even represented in the scriptures—"The father of the faithful." Moses talked with the Lord face to face; received the great moral law, upon the basis of which those of all civilized governments are founded; led Israel forty years, and was taken home to receive the reward of his toils—then Jacob could realize his worth.

Well was the question asked by our Lord, "How can the children of the bridechamber mourn while the bridegroom is with them?" It is said, that he travelled and taught the righteous principles of his kingdom three years, during which he chose twelve men, and ordained them apostles, &c. The people saw and heard—they were particularly benefitted, many of them, by being healed of infirmities and diseases, of plagues, and devils—they saw him walk upon the water—they saw the winds and waves calmed at his command—they saw thousands fed to the full with a pittance, and the very powers of darkness tremble in his presence, and like others before them, considered it as a dream, or a common occurrence, till the time was fulfilled, and he was offered up. Yet while he was with them he said, you shall desire to see one of the days of the Son of Man and shall not see it.

...

Since the apostles fell asleep all men who profess a belief in the truth of their mission, extol their virtues and celebrate their fame. It seems to have been forgotten that they were men of infirmities and subject to all the feelings, passions, and imperfections common to other men. But it appears that they, as others were before them, are looked upon as men of perfection, holiness, purity, and goodness, far in advance of any since. So were the characters of the prophets held in the days of these apostles.

...

But in reviewing the lives and acts of men in past generations, whenever we find a righteous man among them, there always were excuses for not giving heed or credence to his testimony. The people could see his imperfections; or, if no imperfections, supposed ones, and were always ready to frame an excuse upon that for not believing. No matter how pure the principles, nor how precious the teachings—an excuse was wanted-and an excuse was had.

...

One of two reasons may be assigned as the cause why the messengers of truth have been rejected—perhaps both. The multitude saw their imperfections, or supposed ones, and from that framed an excuse for rejecting them; or else in consequence of the corruption of their own hearts, when reproved, were not willing to repent but sought to make a man an offender for a word, or for wearing camels' hair, eating locusts, drinking wine, or showing friendship to publicans and sinners!

...

You will see that I have made mention of the Messiah, of his mission into the world, and of his walk and outward appearance; but do not understand me as attempting to place him on a level with men, or his mission on a parallel with those of the prophets and apostles—far from this. I view his mission such as none other could fill; that he was offered without spot to God a propitiation for our sins; that he rose triumphant, and victorious over the grave and him that has the power of death.-This, man could not do; it required a perfect sacrifice—man is imperfect; it required a spotless offering—man is not spotless; it required an infinite atonement—man is mortal!

I have, then, as you will see, made mention of our Lord, **to show that individuals teaching truth, whether perfect or imperfect, have been looked upon as the worst of men.** And that even our Savior, the great Shepherd of Israel, was mocked and derided, and placed on a parallel with the prince of devils; and the prophets and apostles, though at this day, looked upon as perfect as perfection, **were considered the basest of the human family by those among whom they lived.** It is not *rumour,* though it is wafted by every gale and reiterated by every zephyr, upon which we are to found our judgments of ones merits or demerits: **If it is, we erect an altar upon which we sacrifice the most perfect of men, and establish a criterion by which the "vilest of the vile" may escape censure.**

...

Chapter 8 – Letter III

December 1834, *Messenger and Advocate*

In Letter III, Oliver comments on the challenge of preserving history. He also emphasizes that he writes about "such facts as are within my knowledge" to counter rumors that enemies of the Church had spread. Oliver explains that the cause of the Church "should be vindicated by laying before the world a correct statement of events as they have transpired from time to time."

Yet this letter introduces some uncertainty because it describes the events in Joseph's life that historians usually associate with Joseph's 1820 vision. Oliver was apparently planning to cover the 1820 vision in Letter IV, but as we'll see, Letter IV switches to Moroni's visit instead.

Oliver skipped a month before publishing Letter IV, possibly because he had to rework it to focus on Moroni's visit instead of the First Vision. I think it was Joseph, not Oliver, who made the editorial decision not to publish the First Vision in these letters. I have proposed that Joseph wasn't ready to publish an account of the First Vision until there was a second witness of the visitation of the Lord, which did not happen until April 3, 1836, when the Savior appeared to Joseph and Oliver together in the Kirtland temple.

In Letter III, Oliver hopes that readers will consider both sides of the matter: "Should I, however, be instrumental in causing a few to hear before they judge, and understand both sides of this matter before they condemn, I shall have the satisfaction of seeing them embrace it, as I am certain that one is the inevitable fruit of the other."

This counsel to avoid a rush to judgment based on one side of a matter is a useful reminder for all of us.

The December 1834 issue of the *Messenger and Advocate* also included a letter from Joseph Smith to Oliver Cowdery that pertained to the series about the history of the Church. It is included in Appendix II.

As explained there, I think Joseph wrote that letter before Letter I was published in October, but Oliver delayed publishing it until after he published Letters I and II for reasons that are apparent when we read those letters. They laid the groundwork for understanding Joseph's letter in the proper context.

Another important event took place in December 1834, the month this letter was published.

On 5 December Joseph ordained Oliver to the office of assistant President of the High and Holy Priesthood of the Church, making President Cowdery higher in rank than Presidents Rigdon and Williams.[25] As we saw previously, when Joseph Smith referred to these letters in his journal, he used the phrase "President Cowdery's letters."

---

[25] http://www.josephsmithpapers.org/paper-summary/account-of-meetings-revelation-and-blessing-5-6-december-1834/1 and http://www.josephsmithpapers.org/paper-summary/journal-1832-1834/94.

LETTER III.

DEAR BROTHER:

After a silence of another month, agreeably to my promise, I proceed upon the subject I proposed in the first No. of the Advocate. Perhaps an apology for brevity may not be improper here, as **many important incidents consequently transpiring in the organization and establishing of a society like the one whose history I am about to give to the world, are overlooked or lost, and soon buried with those who were the actors, will prevent my giving those minute and particular reflections which I have so often wished might have characterized the "acts of the apostles," and the ancient saints.** But such facts as are within my knowledge, will be given without any **reference to inconsistencies in the minds of others,** or impossibilities, in the feelings of such as do not give credence to the system of salvation and redemption, so clearly set forth and so plainly written over the face of the sacred scriptures.

Upon the propriety, then, of a narrative of this kind, I have briefly to remark. **It is known to you that this church has suffered reproach and persecution from a majority of mankind who have heard but a rumor, since its first organization;** and further, you are also conversant with the fact, that no sooner had the messengers of the fulness of the gospel began to proclaim its heavenly precepts, and call upon men to embrace the same, than they were vilified and slandered by thousands who never saw their faces, and much less knew aught derogatory of their characters, moral or religious. Upon this unfair and unsaint-like manner of procedure they have been giving, in large sheets, their own opinions of the incorrectness of our system, and attested volumes of our lives and characters.

Since, then our opposers have been thus kind to introduce our cause before the public, it is no more than just that a correct account

should be given; and since they have invariably sought to cast a shade over the truth, and hinder its influence from gaining ascendancy, it is also proper that **it should be vindicated by laying before the world a correct statement of events as they have transpired from time to time.**

Whether I shall succeed so far in my purpose as to convince the public of the incorrectness of those scurrilous reports which have inundated our land, or even but a small portion of them, will be better ascertained when I close than when I commence; **and I am content to submit it before the candid for perusal, and before the judge of all for inspection, as I most assuredly believe that before HIM I must stand and answer for the deeds transacted in this life.**

Should I, however, be instrumental in causing a few to hear before they judge, and understand both sides of this matter before they condemn, I shall have the satisfaction of seeing them embrace it, as I am certain that one is the inevitable fruit of the other. But to proceed.

You will recollect that I informed you, in my letter published in the first number of the Messenger and Advocate, that **this history would necessarily embrace the life and character of our esteemed friend and brother, J. Smith, jun., one of the presidents of this church**; and for information on that part of the subject, I refer you to his communication of the same, published in this paper; [NOTE: Joseph Smith's letter is included as Appendix II] I shall, therefore, pass over that, till I come to the 15th year of his life.

[NOTE: in subsequent republications, this was changed to the "17th year of his life." The original Letter IV explained that the reference to the 15th year was an error. Oliver's discussion of the Palmyra religious scene, including Rev. Lane's revival and the Smith family's religious views, is omitted.]

66

After strong solicitations to unite with one of those different societies, and seeing the apparent proselyting disposition manifested with equal warmth from each, his [Joseph Smith's] mind was led to more seriously contemplate the importance of a move of this kind.

To profess godliness without its benign influence upon the heart, was thing so foreign from his feelings, that his spirit was not at rest day nor night. To unite with a society professing to be built upon the only sure foundation, and that profession be a vain one, was calculated in its very nature, the more it was contemplated, the more to arouse the mind to the serious consequences of moving hastily in a course fraught with eternal realities. To say he was right, and still be wrong, could not profit; and amid so many, some must be built upon the sand.

In this situation where could he go? If he went to one he was told they were right and all others were wrong—if to another, the same was heard from them. All professed to be the true church, and if not, they were certainly hypocritical; because, if I am presented with a system of religion, and enquire of my teacher whether it is correct, and he informs me that he is not certain, he acknowledges at once that he is teaching without authority, and acting without a commission.

If one professed a degree of authority or preference in consequence of age or right, and that superiority was without evidence, it was insufficient to convince a mind once aroused to that degree of determination which at that time operated upon him. And upon further reflecting, that the Savior had said that the gate was straight, and the way narrow that lead to life eternal, and that few entered there; and that the way was broad, and the gate wide which leadeth to destruction, and that many crowded its current, a proof from some source was wanting to settle the mind and give peace to the agitated bosom. It is not often that the *minds* of men are exercised with proper determination relative to obtaining a certainty of the things of God. They are too apt to rest short of that *assurance* which the Lord Jesus has so freely offered in his word to man, and which so beautifully characterizes his whole plan of salvation, as revealed to us.

[The End}

Chapter 9 – Letter IV

February 1835, *Messenger and Advocate*

Letter IV includes detailed information about Moroni's first visit to Joseph, including his appearance. Alluding to his own experience, Oliver writes, "It is no easy task to describe the appearance of a messenger from the skies."

Oliver says Moroni "gave a history of the aborigines *of this country*," a phrase Joseph later used in the Wentworth letter. It's unclear whether Moroni meant *country* in the sense of a nation (the United States, where Joseph lived), or *country* in the sense of the local area or region. Either way, Moroni was referring to the indigenous people—the Indians—with whom Joseph was familiar and with whom Joseph would have a friendly, close relationship for the rest of his life.

Moroni also told Joseph the record "was *written* and *deposited* not far from that place," meaning where Joseph lived near Palmyra. This means Mormon and Moroni wrote the record while living in what is now western New York.

LETTER IV.

DEAR BROTHER,

In my last I apologized for the brief manner in which I should be obliged to give, in many instances, the history of this church. ... as there are in a great house many vessels, so in the history of a work of this magnitude, many items which would be interesting to those who follow, are forgotten. In fact, I deem every manifestation of the Holy Spirit, dictating the hearts of the saints in the way of righteousness, to be of importance, and this is one reason why I plead an apology.

… **our brother was urged forward and strengthened in the determination to know for himself of the certainty and reality of pure and holy religion**; and it is only necessary for me to say, that while this excitement continued, he continued to call upon the Lord in secret for a full manifestation of divine approbation, and for, to him, the all important information, if a Supreme being did exist, to have an assurance that he was accepted of him. This, most assuredly, was correct—it was right. The Lord has said, long since, and his word remains steadfast, that to him who knocks it shall be opened, and whosoever will, may come and partake of the waters of life freely.

…

On the evening of the 21st of September, 1823, previous to retiring to rest, our brother's mind was unusually wrought up on the subject which had so long agitated his mind; his heart was drawn out in fervent prayer, and his whole soul was so lost to every thing of a temporal nature, that earth to him had lost its charms, and all he desired was to be prepared in heart to commune with some kind messenger who could communicate to him the desired information of his acceptance with God.

At length the family retired, and he, as usual, bent his way, though in silence … he continued still to pray; his heart, though once hard and obdurate, was softened, and that mind which had often flitted, like the "wild bird of passage," had settled upon a determined basis not to be decoyed or driven from its purpose.

In this situation hours passed unnumbered—how many or how few I know not, neither is he able to inform me, but supposes it must have been eleven or twelve and perhaps later, as the noise and bustle of the family in retiring had long since ceased.—While continuing in prayer for a manifestation in some way that his sins were forgiven, endeavoring to exercise faith in the scriptures, on a sudden a light like that of day, only of a purer and far more glorious appearance and brightness, burst into the room; indeed, **to use his own description, the first sight was as though the house was filled with consuming and unquenchable fire.** This sudden appearance of a light so bright as must naturally be expected, occasioned a shock or sensation, visible to the extremities of the body. It was, however, followed with a calmness and serenity of mind, and an overwhelming rapture of joy that surpassed understanding, and in a moment a personage stood before him.

Notwithstanding the room was previously filled with light above the brightness of the sun, as I have before described, yet **there seemed to be an additional glory surrounding or accompanying this personage, which shone with an increased degree of brilliancy, of which he was in the midst; and though his countenance was as lightening, yet it was of a pleasing, innocent and glorious appearance, so much so, that every fear was banished from the heart, and nothing but calmness pervaded the soul.**

It is no easy task to describe the appearance of a messenger from the skies, indeed, I doubt there being an individual clothed with perishable clay, who is capable to do this work. To be sure the Lord appeared to his apostles after his resurrection, and we do not learn as they had not the least difficulty in looking upon him; but from John's description upon Patmos, we learn that he is there represented as most glorious in appearance, and from other items in the sacred scriptures we have the fact recorded where *angels* appeared and conversed with men, and there was no difficulty on the part of the individuals to endure their presence; and others where their glory was so conspicuous that they could not endure. The last description or appearance is the one to which I refer, when I say that it is no easy task to describe their glory.

But it may be well to relate the particulars as far as given: the stature of this personage was a little above the common size of men in this age; his garment was perfectly white, and had the appearance of being without seam.

Though fear was banished from his heart, yet his surprise was no less when he heard him declare himself to be a messenger sent by commandment of the Lord, to deliver a special message, and to witness to him that his sins were forgiven, and that his prayers were heard; and that the scriptures might be fulfilled, which say, "God has chosen the foolish things of the world to confound the things which are mighty; and base things of the world, and things which are despised has God chosen; yea, and things which are not, to bring to nought things which are, that no flesh should glory in his presence. Therefore, says the Lord, I will proceed to do a marvellous work among this people, even a marvellous work and a wonder; the wisdom of their wise shall perish, and the understanding of their prudent shall be hid; for according to his covenant which he made with his ancient saints, his people the house of Israel must come to a knowledge of the gospel, and own that Messiah whom their fathers rejected, and with them the fulness of the Gentiles be gathered in, to rejoice in one fold under one Shepherd.

"This cannot be brought about until first certain preparatory things are accomplished, for so has the Lord purposed in his own mind. He has, therefore, chosen you as an instrument in his hand to bring to light that which shall perform his act, his strange act, and bring to pass a marvelous work and a wonder. Wherever the sound shall go it shall cause the ears of men to tingle, and wherever it shall be proclaimed, the pure in heart shall rejoice, while those who draw near to God with their mouths, and honor him with their lips while their hearts are far from him, will seek its overthrow, and the destruction of those by whose hands it is carried. Therefore, marvel not if your name

72

is made a derision, and had as a by-word among such, if you are the instrument in bringing it, by the gift of God, to the knowledge of the people."

He then proceeded and gave a general account of the promises made to the fathers, and also gave a history of the aborigines of this country, and said they were literal descendants of Abraham. He represented them as once being an enlightened and intelligent people, possessing a correct knowledge of the gospel, and the plan of restoration and redemption. He said **this history was written and deposited not far from that place,** and that it was our brother's privilege, if obedient to the commandments of the Lord, to obtain, and translate the same by the means of the Urim and Thummim, which were deposited for that purpose with the record.

"Yet," said he, "the scripture must be fulfilled before it is translated, which says that the words of a book, which were sealed, were presented to the learned; for thus has God determined to leave men without excuse, and show to the meek that his arm is not shortened that it cannot save."

A part of the book was sealed, and was not to be opened yet. The sealed part, said he, contains the same revelation which was given to John upon the isle of Patmos, and **when the people of the Lord are prepared, and found worthy, then it will be unfolded unto them.**

On the subject of bringing to light the unsealed part of this record, it may be proper to say, that our brother was expressly informed, that it must be done with an eye single to the glory of God; if this consideration did not wholly characterize all his proceedings in relation to it, the adversary of truth would overcome him, or at least prevent his making that proficiency in this glorious work which he otherwise would.

While describing the place where the record was deposited, he gave a minute relation of it, and the vision of his mind being opened at the same time, he was permitted to view it critically; and previously being acquainted with the place, he was able to follow the direction of the vision, afterward, according to the voice of the angel, and obtain the book.

I close for the present by subscribing myself as ever, your brother in Christ.

Chapter 10 – Letter V

March 1835, *Messenger and Advocate*

Letter V contains a discussion of scriptural precedent for divine manifestations and the gathering of Israel. Because it is an interlude between Letters IV and VI, which relate the details of Moroni's visit, it is useful to compare the accounts of Joseph and Oliver concerning that visit.

In Joseph Smith—History 1:36-41, Joseph relates four passages of scripture that Moroni quoted: Malachi 3-4, Isaiah 11, Acts 3:22-23, and Joel 2:28-32. He remembers wording changes that Moroni made, which suggests he made notes at the time or soon thereafter. Any such notes could have been among the "authentic documents" Oliver referred to in his introduction to the letters.

It's also possible Joseph related the details of Moroni's visit to Oliver when they first met in April 1829. Oliver kept a notebook of things Joseph told him. (David Whitmer mentioned the notebook when he arrived in Harmony in 1829 to pick up Joseph and Oliver and take them to Fayette.) Oliver may have used that notebook as a source when he worked with Joseph on these eight historical letters. Oliver's notebook is not extant today; we have no idea what happened to it.

After listing the scriptures Moroni quoted, Joseph says "He [Moroni] quoted many other passages of scripture, and offered many explanations which cannot be mentioned here." (verse 41)

Why couldn't Joseph mention them?

Perhaps he was pressed by time or space, but he may have seen no need to repeat these passages and explanations because the historical letters had already covered them in depth. *Cannot* in verse 41 may really mean *need not.*

Joseph dictated/wrote his history in 1838-9, long after the historical letters were published in the *Messenger and Advocate.* By the time Joseph's history was published in the *Times and Seasons* in 1842, the historical letters had been re-published many times— including the year before in the *Times and Seasons* itself.

Letters IV and VI describe Moroni quoting the following passages. The detail and precision of President Cowdery's account is impressive.

Letter IV (Feb. 1835)
1 Cor. 1:27-29
Isa. 29:14
Isa. 29:13
Isa. 29:11

Letter VI (Apr. 1835)
Psalm 100:1-2
Psalm 107:1-7
Psalm 144:11-12
Joel 2:28
Psalm 144:13
Psalm 146:10
Isa. 1:7
Isa. 1:23-24
Deut. 32:23-24
Isa. 1:25-26

Psalm 107:7
Isa. 2:1-4
Isa. 4:5-6
Jer. 31:27-28
Jer. 31:32-33
Jer. 30:18-21
Jer. 31:1
Jer. 31:8
Isa. 43:6
Jer. 50:4-5
Jer. 31:9
Jer. 31:6
Isa. 2:3
Isa. 11:15-16
Jer. 16:16
Deut. 32:43

LETTER V.

DEAR BROTHER,

You will notice in my last, on rehearsing the words of the angel, where he communicated to our brother, that his sins were forgiven, and that he was called of the Lord to bring to light, by the gift of inspiration, this important intelligence, an item like the following:—"God has chosen the foolish things of the world, and things which are despised, God has chosen;" &c.

This, I conceive to be an important item. Not many mighty and noble, were called in ancient times, because they always *knew so much* that God could not teach them, and a man that would listen to the voice of the Lord and follow the teachings of heaven, always was despised, and considered to be of the foolish class—Paul proves this fact, when he says, "We are made as the filth of the world—the off-scouring of all things unto this day."

I am aware, that a rehearsal of visions, of angels, at this day, is as inconsistent with a portion of mankind as it formerly was, after all the boast of this wise generation in the knowledge of the truth; but there is a uniformity so complete, that on the reflection, one is led to rejoice that it is so.

In my last I gave an imperfect description of the angel, and was obliged to do so, for the reason that my pen would fail to describe an angel in his glory, or the glory of God. I also gave a few sentences which he uttered on the subject of the gathering of Israel, &c. Since writing the former, I have thought it would, perhaps, be interesting to give something more full on this important subject, as well as a revelation of the gospel. That these holy personages should feel a deep interest in the accomplishment

77

of the glorious purposes of the Lord, in his work in the last days, is consistent, when we view critically what is recorded of their sayings in the holy Scriptures.

[A discussion of religious history is omitted.]

In the last days, to fulfill the promises to the ancient prophets, when the Lord is to pour out his Spirit upon all flesh, he has determined to bring to light his gospel to the Gentiles, that it may go to the house of Israel...

But the time has now arrived, in which, according to his covenants, the Lord will manifest to the faithful that he is the same to-day and forever, and that the cup of suffering of his people, the house of Israel, is nearly filled; and that the way may be prepared before their face, he will bring to the knowledge of the people the gospel as it was preached by his servants on this land, and manifest to the obedient the truth of the same, by the power of the Holy Spirit;

[A discussion of scriptures about the gathering is omitted.]

I will give a further detail of the promises to Israel, hereafter, as rehearsed by the angel.

Accept assurance of my esteem as ever.

Chapter 11 – Letter VI

April 1835, *Messenger and Advocate*

Letter VI discusses the gathering of Israel by reference to the Old Testament scriptures Moroni quoted to Joseph Smith. In this excerpt I omitted most of the scriptural and doctrinal references and discussion, but they are worth reviewing in the original. Moroni set out the connection between the Old Testament and the Restoration that LDS authors have followed ever since.

This letter also explains the difficulty of describing everything one learns in visions. President Cowdery explains that prophets know more than they can say, and there is more to be revealed to the Saints in the future.

At one point, he writes, "I believe that the Lord Jesus told many things to his apostles which are not written." President Cowdery may have been thinking about how many times he himself had not written about experiences he and Joseph shared, such as the ministration of Peter, James and John when they conferred the Priesthood.

LETTER VI.

DEAR BROTHER,

I gave, in my last, a few words, on the subject of a few items, as spoken by the angel at the time the knowledge of the record of the Nephites was communicated to our brother, and in consequence of the subject of the gospel and that of the gathering of Israel's being so connected, I found it difficult to speak of the one without mentioning the other; and this may not be improper, as it is evident that the Lord has decreed to bring forth the fulness of the gospel in the last days, previous to gathering Jacob, but a preparatory work, and the other is to follow in quick succession.

This being of so much importance, and of so deep interest to the saints, I have thought best to give a farther detail of the heavenly message, and if I do not give it in the precise words, shall strictly confine myself to the facts in substance.

[Lengthy discussion of the gathering of Israel omitted.]

I have now given you a rehearsal of what was communicated to our brother, when he was directed to go and obtain the record of the Nephites. I may have missed in arrangement in some instances, but the principle is preserved, and you will be able to bring forward abundance of corroborating scripture upon the subject of the gospel and of the gathering. **You are aware of the fact, that to give a minute rehearsal of a lengthy interview with a heavenly messenger, is very difficult, unless one is assisted immediately with the gift of inspiration.**

There is another item I wish to notice on the subject of visions. The Spirit you know, searches all things, even the deep things of God. **When God manifests to his servants those things that are to come, or those which have been, he does it by unfolding them by the power of that Spirit which comprehends all things, always; and so much may be shown and made perfectly plain to the understanding in a short time, that to the world, who are occupied all their life to learn a little, look at the relation of it, and are disposed to call it false.**

You will understand then, by this, that while those glorious things were being rehearsed, the vision was also opened, so that **our brother was**

80

permitted to see and understand much more full and perfect than I am able to communicate in writing.

I know much may be conveyed to the understanding in writing, and many marvellous truths set forth with the pen, but after all it is but a shadow, compared to an open vision of seeing, hearing and realizing eternal things.

And if the fact was known, it would be found, that of all the heavenly communications to the ancients, we have no more in comparison than the alphabet to a quarto vocabulary.

It is said, and I believe the account, that the Lord showed the brother of Jared (Moriancumer) all things which were to transpire from that day to the end of the earth, as well as those which had taken place. I believe that Moses was permitted to see the same, as the Lord caused them to pass in vision before him as he stood upon the mount.

I believe that the Lord Jesus told many things to his apostles which are not written, and after his ascension unfolded all things unto them; I believe that Nephi, the son of Lehi, whom the Lord brought out of Jerusalem, saw the same; I believe that the twelve upon this continent, whom the Lord chose to preach his gospel, when he came down to manifest to this branch of the house of Israel, that he had other sheep who should hear his voice, were also permitted to behold the same mighty things transpire in vision before their eyes; and I believe that the angel Moroni, whose words I have been rehearsing, who communicated the knowledge of the same to the Nephites, in this age, saw also, before he hid up the record unto the Lord, great and marvellous things, which were to transpire when the same should come forth; and I also believe, that God will give line upon line, precept upon precept, to his saints, until all these things will be unfolded to them, and they be finally sanctified and brought into the celestial glory, where tears will be wiped from all faces, and sighing and sorrowing flee away!

May the Lord preserve you from evil and reward you richly for all your afflictions, and crown you in his kingdom. Amen.

Accept, as ever, assurances of the fellowship and esteem of your unworthy brother in the gospel.

Chapter 12 – Letter VII

July 1835, *Messenger and Advocate*

Letter VII contains the critical Cumorah material excerpted in Chapter 5, but it also contains important information about Joseph's spiritual development.

President Cowdery uses the letter to discuss Joseph's deliberations as he experienced the temptation of getting the plates for their monetary value. This is an aspect Joseph never dwelt on in writing, but Oliver could have learned it only from him.

It is possible that Joseph related these thoughts to Oliver in 1835, but by 1835, Joseph seemed more guarded about his inner thoughts, as evidenced by the letter he wrote to Oliver (found in Appendix II). It is also possible—and I think more likely—that Oliver recorded in his notebook what Joseph told him during the translation process in 1829 and then referred to that notebook to write these letters. The notebook is not extant so we will probably never know how Oliver was able to recreate Joseph's thought process in such detail.

Oliver's descriptions of the temptations Joseph faced when he first sought to retrieve the plates from the stone box are significant for several reasons. Joseph and his family were poor. The prospect of gold treasure—over a million dollars' worth in today's money—would have been a tremendous temptation. It took four years for Joseph to overcome the lure of gold riches and prepare himself to obtain the plates.

If Joseph was tempted so deeply by a single set of plates in a stone box, he presumably could not have withstood the temptation of an entire depository full of gold plates and ancient artifacts. This may be the reason Moroni built the separate stone box, in another "department of the hill" as Orson Pratt described it.

Joseph apparently did not learn the location of the depository until he encountered the messenger on the way to Fayette. By that point, he was accustomed to handling golden plates, but surely the idea of much more treasure was an additional test of his faith and self-control.

LETTER VII.

DEAR BROTHER,

You will remember that in my last I brought my subject down to the evening, or night of the 21st of September, 1823, and gave an outline of the conversation of the angel upon the important fact of the blessings, promises and covenants to Israel, and the great manifestations of favour to the world, in the ushering in of the fulness of the gospel, to prepare the way for the second advent of the Messiah, when he comes in the glory of the Father, with the holy angels.

A remarkable fact is to be noticed with regard to this vision. In ancient time the Lord warned some of his servants in dreams: for instance, Joseph, the husband of Mary, was warned in a dream to take the young child and his mother, and flee into Egypt; also, the WISE men were warned of the Lord in a dream not to return to Herod; and when "out of Egypt the Son was called," the angel of the Lord appeared in a dream to Joseph again: also he was warned in a dream to turn aside into the parts of Galilee. Such were the manifestations to Joseph, the favored descendant of the father of the faithful in dreams, and in them the Lord fulfilled his purposes: **But the tone of which I have been speaking is what would have been called an open vision. And though it was in the night, yet it was not a dream. There is no room for conjecture in this matter, and to talk of deception, would be to sport with the common sense of every man who knows when he is awake, when he sees and when he does not see.**

He could not have been deceived in the fact that a being of some kind appeared to him: and that it was an heavenly one, the fulfillment of his words so minutely, up to this time, in addition to the truth and word of salvation which has been developed to this generation, in the Book of Mormon, ought to be conclusive evidence to the mind of every man who is privileged to hear of the same. **He was awake, and in solemn prayer, as you will bear in mind, when the angel made his appearance; from that glory which surrounded him the room was lit up to a perfect brilliancy, so that darkness wholly disappeared: he heard his words with his ears,** and received a joy and happiness indescribable by hearing that his own sins were forgiven, and his former transgressions to be remembered against him no more, if he then continued to walk before the Lord, according to his holy commandments. **He also saw him depart, the light and glory withdraw, leaving a calmness and peace of soul past the language of man to paint. Was he deceived?**

Far from this; for the vision was renewed twice before morning, unfolding further and still further the mysteries of godliness and those things to come. In the morning he went to his labor as usual, but soon the vision of the heavenly messenger was renewed, instructing him to go immediately and view those things of which he had been informed, with a promise that he should obtain them, if he followed the directions and went with an eye single to the glory of God.

Accordingly he repaired to the place which had thus been described. **But it is necessary to give you more fully the express instructions of the angel, with regard to the object of this work in which our brother had now engaged—He was to remember that it was the work of the Lord,** to fulfil certain promises previously made to a branch of the house of Israel of the tribe of Joseph, and when it should be brought forth, it must be done expressly with an eye, as I said before, single to the glory of God, and the welfare and restoration of the house of Israel.

You will understand, then, that no motive of a pecuniary, or earthly nature, was to be suffered to take the lead of the heart of the man thus favored. The allurements of vice, the contaminating influence of wealth, without the direct guidance of the Holy Spirit, must have no place in the heart nor be suffered to take from it that warm desire for the glory and kingdom of the Lord, or, instead of obtaining, disappointment and reproof would most assuredly follow. Such was the instruction and this the caution.

Alternately, as we could naturally expect, the thought of the previous vision was ruminating in his mind, with a reflection of the brightness and glory of the heavenly messenger; but again a thought would start across the mind on the prospects of obtaining so desirable a treasure—one in all *human* probability sufficient to raise him above a level with the common earthly fortunes of his fellow men, and relieve his family from want, in which, by misfortune and sickness they were placed.

It is very natural to suppose that the mind would revolve upon those scenes which had passed, when those who had acquired a *little* of this world's goods, by industry and economy, with the blessings of health or friends, or by art and intrigue, from the pockets of the day-laborer, or the widow and the fatherless, had passed by with a stiff neck and a cold heart, scorning the virtuous because they were poor, and lording over those who were subjected to suffer the miseries of this life.

Alternately did these, with a swift reflection of the words of the holy messenger,—"Remember, that he who does this work, who is thus favoured of the Lord, must do it with his eye single to the glory of the same, and the welfare and restoration of the scattered remnants of the house of Israel"—rush upon his mind with the quickness of electricity. **Here was a struggle indeed; for when he calmly reflected upon his errand, he knew that if God did not give, he could not obtain; and again, with the thought or hope of obtaining, his mind would be carried back to its former reflection of poverty, abuse,—wealth, grandeur and ease, until before arriving at the place described, this wholly occupied his desire; and when he thought upon the fact of what was previously shown him, it was only with an assurance that he should obtain and accomplish his desire in relieving himself and friends from want.**

A history of the inhabitants who peopled this continent, previous to its being discovered to Europeans by Columbus, must be interesting to every man; and as it would develope the important fact, that the present race were descendants of Abraham, and were to be remembered in the immutable covenant of the Most High to that man, and be restored to a knowledge of the gospel, that they, with all nations might rejoice, seemed to inspire further thoughts of gain and income from such a valuable history. Surely, thought he, every man will seize with eagerness, this knowledge, and this incalculable income will be mine. Enough to raise the expectations of any one of like inexperience, placed in similar circumstances. But the important point in this matter is, that man does not see as the Lord, neither are his purposes like his. The small things of this life are but dust in comparison with salvation and eternal life.

It is sufficient to say that such were his reflections during his walk of from two to three miles, the distance from his father's house to the place pointed out. **And to use his own words it seemed as though two invisible powers were influencing, or striving to influence his mind**—one with the reflection that if he obtained the object of his pursuit, it would be through the mercy and condescension of the Lord, and that every act or performance in relation to it, must be in strict accordance with the instruction of that personage who communicated the intelligence to him first; and the other with the thoughts and reflections like those previously mentioned—contrasting his former and present circumstances in life with those to come. That precious instruction recorded on the sacred page—pray always—which was expressly impressed upon him, was at length entirely forgotten, and as I previously remarked, a fixed determination to obtain and aggrandize himself, occupied his mind when he arrived at the place where the record was found.

I must now give you some description of the place where, and the manner in which these records were deposited.

You are acquainted with the mail road from Palmyra, Wayne Co. to Canandaigua, Ontario Co. N. Y. and also, as you pass from the former to the latter place, before arriving at the little village of Manchester, say from three to four, or about four miles from Palmyra, you pass a large hill on the east side of the road. Why I say large, is, because it is as large perhaps, as any in that country. **To a person acquainted with this road, a description would be unnecessary, as it is the largest and rises the highest of any on that route.** The north end rises quite sudden until it assumes a level with the more southerly extremity, and I think I may say an elevation higher than at the south a short distance, say half or three fourths of a mile. As you pass toward Canandaigua it lessens gradually until the surface assumes its common level, or is broken by other smaller hills or ridges, water courses and ravines. **I think I am justified in saying** that this is the highest hill for some distance round, and I am certain that its appearance, as it rises so suddenly from a plain on the north, must attract the notice of the traveller as he passes by.

At about one mile west rises another ridge of less height, running parallel with the former, leaving a beautiful vale between. The soil is of the first quality for the country, and under a state of cultivation, which gives a prospect at once imposing, when one reflects on the fact, that here, between these hills, the entire power and national strength of both the Jaredites and Nephites were destroyed.

By turning to the 529th and 530th pages of the Book of Mormon, you will read Mormon's account of the last great struggle of his people, as they were encamped round this hill Cumorah. (It is printed Camorah, which is an error.) In this valley fell the remaining strength and pride of a once powerful people, the Nephites—once so highly favored of the Lord, but at that time in darkness, doomed to suffer extermination by the hand of their barbarous and uncivilized brethren. From the top of this hill, Mormon, with a few others, after the battle, gazed with horror upon the mangled remains of those who, the day before, were filled with anxiety, hope, or doubt. A few had fled to the South, who were hunted down by the victorious party, and all who would not deny the Savior and his religion, were put to death. Mormon himself, according to the record of his son Moroni, was also slain.

But a long time previous to this national disaster it appears from his own account, he foresaw approaching destruction. In fact, if he perused the records of his fathers, which were in his possession, he could have learned that such would be the case. Alma, who lived before the coming of the Messiah, prophesies this. He however, by Divine appointment, abridged from those records, in his own style and language, a short account of the more important and prominent items, from the days of Lehi to his own time, after which he deposited, as he says, on the 529th page, all the records in this same hill, Cumorah, and after gave his small record to his son Moroni, who, as appears from the same, finished it, after witnessing the extinction of his people as a nation.

It was not the wicked who overcame the righteous: far from this: it was the wicked against the wicked, and by the wicked the wicked were punished. The Nephites who were once enlightened, had fallen from a more elevated standing as to favour and privilege before the Lord, in consequence of the righteousness of their fathers, and now falling below, for such was actually the case, were suffered to be overcome, and the land was left to the possession of the red men, who were without intelligence, only in the affairs of their wars; and **having no records, only preserving their history by tradition from father to son, lost the account of their true origin, and wandered from river to river, from hill to hill, from mountain to mountain, and from sea to sea,** till the land was again peopled, in a measure, by a rude, wild, revengeful, warlike and barbarous race. Such are our Indians.

This hill, by the Jaredites, was called Ramah: by it, or around it, pitched the famous army of Coriantumr their tent. Coriantumr was the last king of the Jaredites. **The opposing army were to the west, and in this same valley, and near by.** From day to day, did that mighty race spill their blood, in wrath, contending as it were, brother against brother, and father against son. **In this same spot, in full view from the top of this same hill, one may gaze with astonishment upon the ground which was twice covered with the dead and dying of our fellowmen.**

Here may be seen, where once sunk to nought the pride and strength of two mighty nations; and here may be contemplated in solitude, while nothing but the faithful record of Mormon and Moroni is now extant to inform us of the fact, scenes of misery and distress—the aged, whose silver locks in other places, and at other times, would command reverence; the mother, who, in other circumstances would be spared from violence— the infant, whose tender cries would be regarded and listened to with a feeling of compassion and tenderness— and the virgin, whose grace, beauty and modesty, would be esteemed and held inviolate by all good men and enlightened and civilized nations, were alike disregarded and treated with scorn! In vain did the hoary head and man of gray hairs ask for mercy—in vain did the mother plead for compassion—in vain did the helpless and harmless infant weep for very anguish—and in vain did the virgin seek to escape the ruthless hand of revengeful foes and demons in human form—all alike were trampled down by the feet of the strong, and crushed beneath the rage of battle and war! Alas! who can reflect upon the last struggles of great and populous nations, sinking to dust beneath the hand of justice and retribution, without weeping over the corruption of the human heart, and sighing for the hour when the clangor of arms shall no more be heard, nor the calamities of contending armies be any more experienced for a thousand years? Alas! the calamity of war, the extinction of nations, the ruin of kingdoms, the fall of empires, and the dissolution of governments! Oh! the misery, distress and evil attendant, on these. Who can contemplate like scenes without sorrowing, and who so destitute of commiseration as not to be pained that man has fallen so low, so far beneath the station in which he was created?

In this vale lie commingled, in one mass of ruin, the ashes of thousands, and in this vale were destined to be consumed the fair forms and vigorous systems of tens of thousands of the human race—blood mixed with blood, flesh with flesh, bones with bones, and dust with dust! When the vital spark which animated their clay had fled, each lifeless lump lay on one common level—cold and inanimate. Those bosoms which had burned with rage against each other for real or supposed injury, had now ceased to heave with malice; those arms which were a few moments before nerved with strength, had alike become paralyzed, and those hearts which had been fired with revenge, had now ceased to heave with malice; those arms which were a few moments before nerved with strength, had alike become paralyzed, and those hearts which had been fired with revenge, had now ceased to beat, and the head to think—in silence, in solitude, and in disgrace alike, they have long since turned to earth, to their mother dust, to await the august, and to millions, awful hour, when the trump of the Son of God shall echo and re-echo from the skies, and they come forth quickened and immortalized, to not only stand in each other's presence, but before the bar of him who is Eternal!

With sentiments of pure respect, I conclude by subscribing myself your brother in the gospel.

Chapter 13 – Letter VIII

October 1835, *Messenger and Advocate*

Letter VIII, the last in the series, continues the description of Cumorah, focusing on the details of the stone box Moroni constructed. Here, Oliver spells out the difference between fact and speculation.

"How far below the surface these records were placed by Moroni, I am unable to say... However, on this point I shall leave every man to draw his own conclusion and form his own speculation, as I only promised to give a description of the place at the time the records were found in 1823."

Those who claim Oliver merely speculated in Letter VII about the scene of the last battles, or the location of Mormon's depository, ignore how carefully Oliver differentiated between speculation and facts. Throughout these letters, Oliver emphasized he was relating facts within his knowledge (or the knowledge of Joseph Smith).

When he didn't know a fact, such as how deep Moroni originally buried the stone box, he explained his thinking clearly and allowed his readers to make up their own minds.

Oliver also describes more of the interaction between Joseph and Moroni.

Later in the letter, Oliver returns to his defense of the character of Joseph Smith and his family.

LETTER VIII.

DEAR BROTHER,

IN my last I said I should give, partially, a "description of the place where, and the manner in which these records were deposited:" the first promise I have fulfilled, and must proceed to the latter:

The hill of which I have been speaking, at the time mentioned, presented a varied appearance: the north end rose suddenly from the plain, forming a promontory without timber, but covered with grass. As you passed to the south you soon came to scattering timber, the surface having been cleared by art or by wind; and a short distance further left, you are surrounded with the common forest of the country.

It is necessary to observe, that even the part cleared was only occupied for pasturage, its steep ascent and narrow summit not admitting the plow of the husbandman with any degree of ease or profit. **It was at the second mentioned place where the record was found to be deposited, on the west side of the hill, not far from the top down its side; and when myself visited the place in the year 1830, there were several trees standing: enow [enough] to cause a shade in summer, but not so much as to prevent the surface being covered with grass—which was also the case when the record was first found.**

Whatever may be the feeling of men on the reflection of past acts which have been performed on certain portions or spots of this earth, I know not, neither does it add or diminish to nor from the reality of my subject. When Moses heard the voice of God, at the foot of Horeb, out of the burning bush, he was commanded to take his shoes off his feet, for the ground on which he stood was holy. The same may be observed when

Joshua beheld the "Captain of the Lord's host" by Jerico. And I confess that my mind was filled with many reflections; and though I did not *then* loose my shoe, yet with gratitude to God did I offer up the sacrifice of my heart.

How far below the surface these records were placed by Moroni, I am unable to say; but from the fact that they had been some fourteen hundred years buried, and that too on the side of a hill so steep, one is ready to conclude that they were some feet below, as the earth would naturally wear more or less in that length of time. But they being placed toward the top of the hill, the ground would not remove as much as two-thirds, perhaps. Another circumstance would prevent a wearing of the earth: in all probability, as soon as timber had time to grow, the hill was covered, after the Nephites were destroyed, and the roots of the same would hold the surface. **However, on this point I shall leave every man to draw his own conclusion and form his own speculation, as I only promised to give a description of the place at the time the records were found in 1823.**

It is sufficient for my present purpose, to know that such is the fact, that in 1823, yes, 1823, a man with whom I have had the most intimate and personal acquaintance, for almost seven years, actually discovered by the vision of God, the plates from which the Book of Mormon, as much as it is disbelieved, was translated! Such is the case, though men rack their very brains to invent falsehoods, and then waft them upon every breeze, to the contrary notwithstanding.

I have now given sufficient on the subject of the hill Cumorah—it has a singular and imposing appearance for that country, and must excite the curious enquiry of every lover of the Book of Mormon, though, I hope, never like Jerusalem and the sepulchre of our Lord, the pilgrims. **In my estimation, certain places are dearer to me for what they *now* contain, than for what they *have* contained.** For the satisfaction of such as believed I have been thus particular, and to avoid the question being a thousand times asked, more than any other cause, shall proceed and be as particular as heretofore.

The manner in which the plates were deposited. First, a hole of sufficient depth, (how deep I know not,) was dug. At the bottom of this was laid a stone of suitable size, the upper surface being smooth. At each edge was placed a large quantity of cement, and into this cement, at the four edges of this stone were placed erect, four others, *their* bottom edges resting *in* the cement at the outer edges of the first stone. The four last named, when placed erect, formed a box, the corners, or where the edges of the four came in contact, were also cemented so firmly that the moisture from without was prevented from entering.

It is to be observed, also, that the inner surface of the four erect, or side stones was smooth. This box was sufficiently large to admit a breast-plate, such as was used by the ancients to defend the chest, &c., from the arrows and weapons of their enemy. From the bottom of the box, or from the breast-plate, arose three small pillars composed of the same description of cement used on the edges; and upon these three pillars was placed the record of the children of Joseph, and of a people who left the tower far, far before the days of Joseph, or a sketch of each, which had it not been for this, and the never failing goodness of God, *we* might have perished in our sins, having been left to bow down before the altars of the Gentiles, and to have paid homage to the priests of Baal! I must not forget to say that this box, containing the record was covered with another stone, the bottom surface being flat and the upper, crowning. But those three pillars were not so lengthy as to cause the plates and the crowning stone to come in contact.

I have now given you, according to my promise, the manner in which this record was deposited; though when it was first visited by our brother, in 1823, a part of the crowning stone was visible above the surface, while the edges were concealed by the soil and grass, from which circumstance you will see, that however deep this box might have been placed by Moroni at first, the time had been sufficient to wear the earth so that it was easily discovered, when once directed, and yet not enough to make a *perceivable* difference to the passer by. So wonderful are the works of the Almighty, and so far from our finding out are his ways, that one who trembles to take his holy name into his lips, is left to wonder at his exact providences, and the fulfilment of his purposes in the event of times and seasons.

A few years sooner might have found even the top stone concealed, and discouraged our brother from attempting to make a further trial to obtain this rich treasure, for fear of discovery; and a few later might have left the small box uncovered, and exposed its valuable contents to the rude calculations and vain speculations of those who neither understand common language nor fear God. But such would have been contrary to the words of the ancients and the promises made to them; and this is why I am left to admire the works and see the wisdom in the designs of the Lord in all things manifested to the eyes of the world: they show that all human inventions are like the vapors, while his word endures forever and his promises to the last generation.

Having thus digressed from my main subject to give a few items for the special benefit of all, it will be necessary to return, and proceed as formerly. And if any suppose I have indulged too freely in reflections, I will only say, that it is my opinion, were one to have a view of the glory of God which is to cover Israel in the last days, and know that these, though they may be thought small things, were the beginning to effect the same, they would be at a loss where to close, should they give a moment's vent to the imaginations of the heart.

You will have wondered, perhaps, that the mind of our brother should be so occupied with the thoughts of the good of this world, at the time of arriving at Cumorah, on the morning of the 22nd of September, 1823, after having been rapt in the visions of heaven during the night, and also seeing and hearing in open day; but the mind of man is easily turned, if it is not held by the power of God through the prayer of faith, and you will remember that I have said that two invisible powers were operating upon his mind during his walk from his residence to Cumorah, and that the one urging the certainly of wealth and ease in this life, had so powerfully wrought upon him, that the great object so carefully and impressively named by the angel, had entirely gone from his recollection that only a fixed determination to obtain now urged him forward.

In this, which occasioned a failure to obtain, at that time, the record, do not understand me to attach blame to our brother: he was young, and his mind easily turned from correct principles, unless he could be favored with a certain round of experience. And yet, while young, untraditionated and untaught in the systems of the world, he was in a situation to be lead into the great work of God, and be qualified to perform it in due time.

After arriving at the repository, a little exertion in removing the soil from the edges of the top of the box, and a light pry, brought to his natural vision its contents. No sooner did he behold this sacred treasure than his hopes were renewed, and he supposed his success certain; and without first attempting to take it from its long place of deposit, he thought, perhaps, there might be something more equally as valuable, and to take only the plates, might give others an opportunity of obtaining the remainder, which could be secure, would still add to his store of wealth.

These, in short, were his reflections, without once thinking of the solemn instruction of the heavenly messenger, that all must be done with an express view of glorying God.

On attempting to take possession of the record a shock was produced upon his system, by an invisible power, which deprived him, in a measure, of his natural strength. He desisted for an instant, and then made another attempt, but was more sensibly shocked than before. What was the occasion of this he knew not—*there* was the pure unsullied record, as had been described—he had heard of the power of enchantment, and a thousand like stories, which held the hidden treasures of the earth, and supposed that physical exertion and personal strength was only necessary to enable him to yet obtain the object of his wish. He therefore made the third attempt with an increased exertion, when his strength failed him more than at either of the former times, and **without premeditating he exclaimed, "Why can I not obtain this book?" "Because you have not kept the commandments of the Lord," answered a voice, within a seeming short distance. He looked, and to his astonishment, there stood the angel, who had previously given him the directions concerning this matter.**

In an instant, all the former instructions, the great intelligence concerning Israel and the last days, were brought to his mind: he thought of the time when his heart was fervently engaged in prayer to the Lord, when his spirit was contrite, and when his holy messenger from the skies unfolded the wonderful things connected with this record. He had come, to be sure, and found the word of the angel fulfilled concerning the reality of the record, but he had failed to remember the great end for which they had been kept, and in consequence could not have power to take them into his possession and bear them away.

At that instant he looked to the Lord in prayer, and **as he prayed darkness began to disperse from his mind and his soul was lit up as it** was the evening before, and he was filled with the Holy Spirit; and again did the Lord manifest his condescension and mercy: the heavens were opened and the glory of the Lord shone round about and rested upon him.

While he thus stood gazing and admiring, the angel said, "Look!" and as he thus spake he beheld the prince of darkness, surrounded by his innumerable train of associates. All this passed before him, and the heavenly messenger said, "All this is shown, the good and the evil, the holy and impure, the glory of God and the power of darkness, that you may know hereafter the two powers and never be influenced or overcome by that wicked one. Behold, whatever entices and leads to good, and to do good, is of God, and whatever does not is of that wicked one. It is he that fills the hearts of men with evil, to walk in darkness and blaspheme God; and you may learn from henceforth, that his ways are to destruction, but the way of holiness is peace and rest.

You now see why you could not obtain this record; that the commandment was strict, and that if ever these sacred things are obtained, they must be by prayer and faithfulness in obeying the Lord. They are not deposited here for the sake of accumulating gain and wealth for the glory of this world; they were sealed by the prayer of faith, and because of the knowledge which they contain, they are of no worth among the children of men, only for their knowledge. On them is contained the fulness of the gospel of Jesus Christ, as it was given to his people on this land, and when it shall be brought forth by the power of God it shall be carried to the Gentiles, of whom many will receive it, and after will the seed of Israel be brought into the fold of their Redeemer by obeying it also.

Those who kept the commandments of the Lord on this land, desired this at his hand, and through the prayer of faith obtained the promise, that if their descendants should transgress and fall away, that a record might be kept, and in the last days come to their children. These things are sacred, and must be kept so, for the promise of the Lord concerning them must be fulfilled.

No man can obtain them if his heart is impure, because they contain that which is sacred; and, besides, should they be entrusted in unholy hands the knowledge could not come to the world, because they cannot be interpreted by the learning of this generation; consequently, they would be considered of no worth, only as precious metal.

Therefore, remember, that they are to be translated by the gift and power of God.

By them will the Lord work a great and a marvelous work: the wisdom of the wise shall become as nought, and the understanding of the prudent shall be hid, and because the power of God shall be displayed, those who profess to know the truth, but walk in deceit, shall tremble with anger; but with signs and with wonders, with gifts and with healings, with the manifestations of the power of God, and with the Holy Ghost, shall the hearts of the faithful be comforted. You have now beheld the power of God manifested and the power of Satan: you see that there is nothing that is desirable in the works of darkness; that they cannot bring happiness; that those who are overcome therewith are miserable, while, on the other hand, the righteous are blessed with a place in the kingdom of God, where joy unspeakable surrounds them.

There they rest beyond the power of the enemy of truth, where no evil can disturb them. The glory of God crowns them, and they continually feast upon his goodness and enjoy his smiles. Behold, notwithstanding you have seen this great display of power, by which you may ever be able to detect the evil one, yet I give unto you another sign, and when it comes to pass then know that the Lord is God, and that he will fulfil his purposes, and that the knowledge which this record contains will go to every nation, and kindred, and tongue, and people under the whole heaven.

This is the sign: When these things begin to be known, that is, when it is known that the Lord has shown you these things, the workers of iniquity will seek your overthrow: they will circulate falsehoods to destroy your reputation, and also will seek to take your life; but remember this if you are faithful, and shall hereafter continue to keep the commandments of the Lord, you shall be preserved to bring these things forth; for in due time he will again give you a commandment to come and take them.

When they are interpreted, the Lord will give the holy priesthood to some, and they shall begin to proclaim this gospel and baptize by water, and after that they shall have power to give the Holy Ghost by the laying on of their hands. Then will persecution rage more and more; for the iniquities of men shall be revealed, and those who are not built upon the Rock will seek to overthrow this Church; **but it will increase the more opposed, and spread further and further, increasing in knowledge till they shall be sanctified and receive an inheritance where the glory of God will rest upon them;** and when this takes place, and all things are prepared, the ten tribes of Israel will be revealed in the north country, whither they have been for a long season; and when this is fulfilled will be brought to pass that saying of the prophet—"And the Redeemer shall come to Zion, and unto them that turn from transgression in Jacob, saith the Lord" But, notwithstanding the workers of iniquity shall seek your destruction the arm of the Lord will be extended and you will be borne off conqueror, if you keep all his commandments.

Your name shall be known among the nations, for the work which the Lord will perform by your hands shall cause the righteous to rejoice and the wicked to rage: with the one it shall be had in honor, and with the other in reproach; yet, with these it shall be a terror because of the great and marvelous work which shall follow the coming forth of this fulness of the gospel.

Now, go thy way, remembering what the Lord has done for thee, and be diligent in keeping his commandments, and he will deliver thee from temptations and all the arts and devices of the wicked one. Forget not to pray, that thy mind may become strong that when he shall manifest unto thee, thou mayest have power to escape the evil, and obtain these precious things."

Though I am unable to paint before the mind, a perfect description of the scenery which passed before our brother, I think I have said enough to give you a field for reflection which may not be unprofitable. You see the great wisdom in God in leading him thus far, that his mind might begin to be more matured, and thereby be able to judge correctly, the spirits. I do not say that he would not have obtained the record had he gone according to the direction of the angel—I say that he would; but God knowing all things from the beginning, began thus to instruct his servant. And in this it is plainly to be seen that the adversary of truth is not sufficient to overthrow the work of God.

You will remember that I said, two invisible powers were operating upon the mind of our brother while going to Cumorah. **In this, then, I discover wisdom in the dealings of the Lord: it was impossible for any man to translate the book of Mormon by the gift of God, endure the afflictions, and temptations, and devices of Satan, without being overthrown, unless he had been previously benefitted with a certain round of experience:** and had our brother obtained the record the first time, not knowing how to detect the works of darkness, he might have been deprived of the blessing of sending forth the word of truth to this generation.

Therefore, God knowing that Satan would thus lead his mind astray, began at that early hour, that when the full time should arrive, he might have a servant prepared to fulfil his purpose. So, however afflicting to his feelings this repulse might have been, he had reason to rejoice before the Lord, and be thankful for the favors and mercies shown: that whatever other instruction was necessary to the accomplishing this great work, he had learned, by experience, how to discern between the spirit of Christ and the spirit of the devil.

From this time to September, 1827, few occurrences worthy of note, transpired. As a fact to be expected, nothing of importance could be recorded concerning a generation in darkness. In the mean time our brother of whom I have been speaking, passed the time as others, in laboring for his support. But in consequence of certain false and slanderous reports which have been circulated, justice would require me to say something upon the private life of one whose character has been so shamefully traduced.

By some he is said to have been a lazy, idle, vicious, profligate fellow. These I am prepared to contradict, and that too by the testimony of *many* persons with whom I have been intimately acquainted, and know to be individuals of the strictest veracity, and unquestionable integrity. All these strictly and virtually agree in saying, that he was an honest, upright, virtuous, and faithfully industrious young man. And those who say to the contrary can be influenced by no other motive than to destroy the reputation of one who never injured any man in either property or person.

While young, I have been informed he was afflicted with sickness; but I have been told by those for whom he has labored, that he was a young man of truth and industrious habits. And I will add further that it is my conviction, if he never had been called to the exalted station in which he now occupies, he might have passed down the stream of time with ease and in respectability, without the foul and hellish tongue of slander ever being employed against him. It is no more than to be expected, I admit, that men of corrupt hearts will try to traduce his character and put a stop upon his name: indeed, this is according to the word of the angel; but this does not prohibit me from speaking freely of his merits, and contradicting those falsehoods—I feel myself bound so to do, and I know that my testimony, on this matter, will be received and believed while those who testify to the contrary are crumbled to dust, and their words swept away in the general mass of lies, when God shall purify the earth!

Connected with this, is the character of the family: and on this I say as I said concerning the character of our brother—I feel myself bound to defend the innocent always when opportunity offers. Had not those who are notorious for lies and dishonesty, also assailed the character of the family, I should pass over them here in silence; but now I shall not forbear.

It has been industriously circulated that they were dishonest, deceitful and vile. **On this I have the testimony of responsible persons, who have said and will say, that this is basely false; and besides, a personal acquaintance for seven years, has demonstrated that all the difficulty is, they were once poor, (yet industrious,) and have now, by the help of God, arisen to note, and their names are like to, (indeed they will,) be handed down to posterity, and had among the righteous. They are industrious honest, virtuous and liberal to all.**

This is their character; and though many take advantage of their liberality, God will reward *them*; but this is the fact, and this testimony shall shine upon the records of the Saints, and be recorded on the archives of heaven to be read in the day of eternity, when the wicked and perverse, who have vilely slandered them without cause or provocation, reap their reward with the unjust, where there is weeping, wailing and gnashing of teeth—if they do not repent.

Soon after this visit to Cumorah, a gentleman from the south part of the State, (Chenango County,) employed our brother as a common labourer, and accordingly he visited that section of the country; and had he not been accused of digging down all, or nearly so, the mountains of Susquehannah, or causing others to do it by some art of necromancy, I should leave this, for the present, unnoticed.

You will remember, in the mean time, that those who seek to vilify his character, say that he has always been notorious for his idleness. This gentleman, whose name is Stowell, resided in the town of Bainbridge, on or near the head waters of the Susquehannah river. Some forty miles south, or down the river, in the town of Harmony, Susquehannah county, Pa. is said to be a cave or subterraneous recess, whether entirely formed by art or not I am uninformed, neither does this matter; but such is said to be the case,—when a company of Spaniards, a long time since, when the country was uninhabited by white settlers, excavated from the bowels of the earth ore, and coined a large quantity of money; after which they secured the cavity and evacuated, leaving a part still in the cave, purposing to return at some distant period. A long time elapsed and this account came from one of the individuals who was first engaged in this mining business.

The country was pointed out and the spot minutely described. This, I believe, is the substance, so far as my memory serves, though I shall not pledge my veracity for the correctness of the account as I have given. Enough however, was credited of the Spaniard's story, to excite the belief of many that there was a fine sum of the precious metal being coined in this subterraneous vault, among whom was our employer; and accordingly our brother was required to spend a few months with some others in excavating the earth, in pursuit of this treasure.

While employed here, he became acquainted with the family of Isaac Hale, of whom you read in several of the productions of those who have sought to destroy the validity of the book of Mormon. It may be necessary hereafter, to refer you more particularly to the conduct of this family, as their influence has been considerably exerted to destroy the reputation of our brother, probably because he married a daughter of the same, contrary to some of their wishes, and in connexion with this, to certain statements of some others of the inhabitants of that section of country.

But in saying this I do not wish to be understood as uttering aught against Mrs. Smith, (formerly Emma Hale.) She has most certainly evinced a decidedly correct mind and uncommon ability of talent and judgment, in a manifest willingness to fulfil, on her part that passage in sacred writ,—"and they twain shall be one flesh."—by accompanying her husband against the wishes and advice of her relatives, to a land of strangers: and however I may deprecate their actions, can say in justice, *her* character stands as fair for morality, piety and virtue, as any in the world.

Though you may say, this is a digression from the subject proposed, I trust I shall be indulged, for the purpose of satisfying many, who have heard so many slanderous reports that they are lead to believe them true because they are not contradicted; and besides, *this* generation are determined to oppose every item in the form or under the pretence of revelation, unless it comes through a man who has always been more pure than Michael the great prince; and as this is the fact, and my opposers have put me to the necessity, I shall be more prolix, and have no doubt, before I give up the point, shall prove to your satisfaction, and to that of every man, that the translator of the book of Mormon is worthy the appellation of a seer and a prophet of the Lord.

In this I do not pretend that he is not a man subject to passion like other men, beset with infirmities and encompassed with weaknesses; but if he is, all men were so before him, and a pretence to the contrary would argue a more than mortal, which would at once destroy the whole system of the religion of the Lord Jesus; for he anciently chose the weak to overcome the strong, the foolish to confound the wise, (I mean considered so by this world,) and by the foolishness of preaching to save those who believe.

On the private character of our brother I need add nothing further at present, previous to his obtaining the records of the Nephites, only that while in that country, some very officious person complained of him as a disorderly person, and brought him before the authorities of the county; but there being no cause of action he was honorably acquitted. From this time forward he continued to receive instruction concerning the coming forth of the fulness of the gospel, from the mouth of the heavenly messenger, until he was directed to visit again the place where the records was deposited.

For the present I close, with a thankful heart that I am permitted to see thousands rejoicing in the assurance of the promises of the Lord, confirmed unto them through the obedience of the everlasting covenant.

As ever your brother in the Lord Jesus.

Chapter 14 – Conclusion

Appendix III contains comments about Cumorah by Joseph Fielding Smith, who was both Church Historian and a member of the Quorum of the Twelve Apostles at the time. President Smith made a strong case for Cumorah. Now the Joseph Smith Papers have given us even more information than he had.

For example, President Smith noted that Letter VII was originally published in the *Messenger and Advocate* and republished in the *Times and Seasons*. However, he did not mention other reprintings in the *Millennial Star*, in Orson Pratt's pamphlet, in the *Gospel Reflector*, in the 1844 pamphlet published in Edinburgh, in *The Prophet*, or in the *Improvement Era*.

People often ask if the Church has an official position on Book of Mormon geography. Members are free to study the issue and reach their own conclusions, but the prophets and apostles have consistently and repeatedly taught two things: (i) Cumorah is in New York, and (ii) we don't know where the other Book of Mormon events took place.

The Church has guidelines about official doctrine.[26] One element is whether the teaching is "consistently proclaimed in official Church publications," As we've seen, and as President Smith related, that element has been satisfied with these eight letters.

The other element is whether the teaching originated with the First Presidency and Quorum of the Twelve.

---

[26] See https://www.mormonnewsroom.org/article/approaching-mormon-doctrine

The letters originated with the First Presidency as the joint effort of President Joseph Smith and President Oliver Cowdery. Presidents Sidney Rigdon and Frederick G. Williams later endorsed the letters. The Quorum of the Twelve Apostles at the time, including Brigham Young, Heber C. Kimball, and Orson and Parley P. Pratt, also affirmed the New York Cumorah throughout their lives, as have subsequent prophets and apostles such as James E. Talmage, LeGrand Richards, and Marion G. Romney.

The intellectuals who reject Letter VII claim President Cowdery and the other prophets who have taught the New York Cumorah were merely expressing their incorrect opinions. President Ezra Taft Benson warned of this when he said, "The learned may feel the prophet is only inspired when he agrees with them, otherwise the prophet is just giving his opinion—speaking as a man."

Those interested in knowing more can read my blogs on the topic, particularly www.lettervii.com. (My blogs are listed at the front of this book on p. ii.)

Regardless of one's personal opinion about the location of Cumorah, every member of the Church today should read Letter VII, just as members of the Church were reading it when Joseph Smith was alive. It's an important part of our history. It was ubiquitous among early Church members and guided their thinking about the Book of Mormon.

To be fully informed, Church members should also read the teachings of the other prophets about the New York Cumorah, such as President Marion G. Romney's address in General Conference titled "America's Destiny." This is available on lds.org at https://www.lds.org/general-conference/1975/10/americas-destiny?lang=eng

What we do with this information is up to us as individuals.

Appendix I: Detailed Timeline

April-June 1829. Oliver arrives in Harmony, Pennsylvania, and acts as scribe while Joseph translates and dictates the Book of Mormon.

April 1829. Oliver tries to translate, fails, and is told by the Lord that "I would that ye should continue until you have finished this record... And then behold, other records have I, that I will give unto you power that you may assist to translate." D&C 9:1-2

April 1829. At some point, Joseph and Oliver consider retranslating the lost 116 pages (the Book of Lehi). Instead, the Lord tells them to "continue on unto the finishing of the remainder of the work of translation as you have begun... [but] you shall not translate again those words which have gone forth out of your hands." D&C 10:3, 30. Instead, the Lord says, "you shall translate the engravings which are on the plates of Nephi." But Joseph doesn't have the plates of Nephi yet. They were not part of the plates in Moroni's stone box. Instead, these plates are the "other records" to which the Lord referred in D&C 9. Joseph will not receive the plates of Nephi until he arrives in Fayette in June.

May 15, 1829. Joseph and Oliver receive the Aaronic priesthood from John the Baptist.

May 1829. Joseph and Oliver complete the translation of the Harmony plates by translating the last leaf of the plates—the Title Page. They write to David Whitmer, asking him to take them to Fayette.

June 1829. Joseph and Oliver receive the Melchizedek priesthood from Peter, James and John.

June 1829. Joseph, Oliver, and David Whitmer meet a divine messenger who is carrying the Harmony plates and says he is headed toward Cumorah (in New York). David had never heard of the place before. Joseph had learned the name from Moroni and Oliver learned it when he wrote it from Joseph's dictation.

June 1829. Joseph, Oliver, David and Martin Harris see the plates, shown to them by an angel. Oliver and David are told they will select the first twelve apostles. (D&C 18)

1829-1830. On multiple occasions, Oliver, Joseph and others, including Joseph's brothers Hyrum and Don Carlos, visit the room in the hill that contains the Mormon's depository of Nephite records and other artifacts. (See discussion about Brigham Young below.) At some point they move everything to another location, possibly back to the Hill Shim.

April 1830. The Church is organized, Oliver is named an apostle of Jesus Christ and the second elder of the Church (D&C 20). Joseph and Oliver are sustained as the presiding officers of the church and ordain one another. (D&C 21).

July 1830. Oliver is called to preach: "And thy brother Oliver shall continue in bearing my name before the world, and also to the church. And he shall not suppose that he can say enough in my cause; and lo, I am with him to the end." (D&C 24:10)

Sept. 1830. Oliver is told he shall be heard by the Church: " Behold, I say unto thee, Oliver, that it shall be given unto thee that thou shalt be heard by the church in all things whatsoever thou shalt teach them by the Comforter, concerning the revelations and commandments which I have given." (D&C 28:1) This same revelation instructs Oliver to preach the gospel to the Lamanites—the Indians in New York and Ohio.

1831-1833. Oliver serves various missions, trips to Missouri, working in Kirtland, etc.

Nov. 1832. Joseph starts his first journal (Journal, 1832-1834) that is partly written in his handwriting, as well the writing of Oliver, Sidney Rigdon, and Frederick G. Williams. It is available online at this link: http://josephsmithpapers.org/paperSummary/?target=X3702#!/paperSummary/journal-1832-1834&p=2)

29 Oct 1834. After prior incomplete efforts to write his history, Joseph helps Oliver write a series of letters that will become part of Joseph's history (as Welch observed in the above quotation). Oliver introduces his series of letters with this statement in the Oct 1834 *Messenger and Advocate*: "That our narrative may be correct, and particularly the introduction, it is proper to inform our patrons, that our brother J. SMITH jr. has offered to assist us. Indeed, there are many items connected with the fore part of this subject that render his labor indispensable. With his labor and with authentic documents now in our possession, we hope to render this a pleasing and agreeable narrative, well worth the examination and perusal of the Saints.-To do justice to this subject will require time and space: we therefore ask the forbearance of our readers, **assuring them that it shall be founded upon facts.**"

5 Dec. 1834. Joseph ordains Oliver as Assistant President of the Church, a position senior to Joseph's counselors in the First Presidency.

July 1835. Oliver publishes **Letter VII** in the *Messenger and Advocate*, unequivocally identifying the New York Cumorah as the scene of the last battles of Jaredites and Nephites.

October 1835. Joseph directs his scribes to copy Oliver's letters into his journal as part of "a history of my life." President Frederick G. Williams of the First Presidency begins the transcription before another scribe takes over.

April 3, 1836. The Lord appears to Joseph and Oliver in the Kirtland temple, along with Moses, Elias, and Elijah.

1840. Parley P. Pratt publishes some of the letters, including **Letter VII**, in the *Millennial Star* in England. His brother Orson Pratt publishes parts of **Letters VII and VIII** in *Interesting Account of Several Remarkable Visions*.

March 1841. Benjamin Winchester republishes Oliver's letters in the *Gospel Reflector*, having obtained express permission from Joseph to do so.

April 1841. Don Carlos republishes Oliver's **Letter VII** in the *Times and Seasons.*

1844. In response to frequent solicitation, President Cowdery's letters, including **Letter VII** are published in Liverpool, England, in a pamphlet titled "Letters of Oliver Cowdery to W.W. Phelps, on the Origin of the Book of Mormon and the Rise of the Church of Jesus Christ of Latter-day Saints."

June 1844. William Smith, Joseph's brother, takes over as editor of *The Prophet,* a Mormon newspaper in New York City. Two days after the martyrdom in Carthage, *The Prophet* publishes Letter **VII**.

June 17, 1877. Two months before his death, Brigham Young discusses Cumorah at a special conference in Farmington, Utah:

"**This is an incident in the life of Oliver Cowdery, but he did not take the liberty of telling such things in meeting as I take.** I tell these things to you, and I have a motive for doing so. **I want to carry them to the ears of my brethren and sisters, and to the children also,** that they may grow to an understanding of some things that seem to be entirely hidden from the human family. **Oliver Cowdery went with the Prophet Joseph when he deposited these plates...** Oliver says that when Joseph and Oliver went there, the hill opened, and they walked into a cave, in which there was a large and spacious room.... [1] **I tell you this as coming not only from Oliver Cowdery, but others who were familiar with it, and who understood it just as well as we understand coming to this meeting,** enjoying the day, and by and by we separate and go away, forgetting most of what is said, but remembering some things... **I relate this to you, and I want you to understand it. I take this liberty of referring to those things so that they will not be forgotten and lost.** Carlos Smith was a young man of as much veracity as any young man we had, and he was a witness to these things...."

[NOTE: FairMormon reports on this but omits everything after [1] above and follows it with the assertion that the experience "was most likely a vision, or a divine transportation to another locale."]

1899. The Church magazine *The Improvement Era* publishes President Cowdery's historical letters, including Letter VII. Joseph F. Smith is the editor.

1928. The Church purchases the Hill Cumorah in New York. In General Conference on April 6, 1928, President Anthony W. Ivins of the First Presidency declares the following facts: "That the hill Cumorah, and the hill Ramah are identical. That it was **around this hill** that the armies of both the Jaredites and Nephites fought their great last battles. That it was **in this hill** that Mormon deposited all of the sacred records which had been entrusted to his care by Ammaron, except the abridgment which he had made from the plates of Nephi, which were delivered into the hands of his son, Moroni. We know positively that it was **in this hill** that Moroni deposited the abridgment made by his father, and his own abridgment of the record of the Jaredites, and that it was **from this hill** that Joseph Smith obtained possession of them."

1938. Joseph Fielding Smith evaluated the evidence and wrote, "This former scene of strife and bloodshed, where two nations perished, later the sacred repository of ancient records, today is the abode of peaceful cattle, reclining and chewing the cud. [Note: See discussion in Appendix III below.]

1960s. Sidney Sperry begins thinking Cumorah is in "Middle America" meaning Mesoamerica, apparently due to the limited geography theory and the anonymous 1842 *Times and Seasons* articles.

1975. In October General Conference, President Marion G. Romney reaffirmed the New York Cumorah. With five Presidents of the Church in attendance (Spencer W. Kimball, Ezra Taft Benson, Howard W. Hunter, Gordon B. Hinckley, and Thomas S. Monson), President Romney said, "In the western part of the state of New York near Palmyra is a prominent hill known as the "hill Cumorah." (Morm. 6:6.) On July twenty-fifth of this year, as I stood on the crest **of that hill** admiring with awe the breathtaking panorama which stretched out before me on every hand, my mind reverted to the events which occurred in that vicinity some twenty-five centuries ago—events which brought to an end the great Jaredite nation…. Thus perished **at the foot of Cumorah** the remnant of the once mighty Jaredite nation… the Nephites flourished in America between 600 B.C. and A.D. 400. Their civilization came to an end for the same reason, **at the same place**, and in the same manner as did the Jaredites'… I bear you my personal witness that I know that the things I have presented to you today are true—both those pertaining to past events and those pertaining to events yet to come."

1981. The illustrations in the missionary edition of the Book of Mormon are changed to teach the two-Cumorahs theory instead of the New York Cumorah.

2004. BYU Professor John Clark claims archaeological evidence excludes the New York hill as the real Cumorah. "William Ritchie's [1954] work is telling. He provides a complete archaeological sequence for New York, with nothing missing... I am not an expert on New York archaeology, nor am I likely to be, but I took a few hours to peruse some of the literature and learned that the general course of prehistory outlined for New York fits comfortably and logically with the histories of adjacent regions and that it makes good anthropological sense… When we pay attention to time and to cultural context, it becomes clear that the events described in the Book of Mormon did not occur in New York." [Note: Consider the implications of rejecting the prophets based on taking "a few hours to peruse some of the literature."]

2008. FAIR MORMON (Larry Poulsen) says the hill in New York was "mistakenly named Cumorah by early Saints" because of his interpretation of Book of Mormon geography.

2013. John Sorenson, in *Mormon's Codex* (Deseret Book, 2015), p. 688, writes "There remain Latter-day Saints who insist that the final destruction of the Nephites took place in New York, but any such idea is manifestly absurd. Hundreds of thousands of Nephites traipsing across the Mississippi Valley to New York, pursued (why?) by hundreds of thousands of Lamanites, **is a scenario worthy only of a witless sci-fi movie, not of history.**"

2015. Mesoamerican proponents claim that Joseph merely adopted the tradition incorrectly established by others regarding the New York Cumorah, but the New York hill cannot be the Cumorah described in the text. E.g., Brant A. Gardner, *Traditions of the Fathers* (Greg Kofford Books, 2015), p. 375.

Appendix II: Letter from Joseph Smith to Oliver Cowdery

The first section of the December 1834 *Messenger and Advocate* included an undated letter Joseph wrote to Oliver for publication. (Letter III was published in the second section.)

The letter is important for the biographical material it contains, but also because it has raised a question about how involved Joseph actually was in writing these letters.

Joseph began the letter by writing this:

Brother O Cowdery:
Having learned from the first No. of the Messenger and Advocate, that you were, not only about to "give a history of the rise and progress of the church of the Latter Day Saints;" but, that said "history would necessarily embrace my life and character," I have been induced to give you the time and place of my birth…"

At first glance, this letter raises an inference that Joseph did not know about Oliver's intentions until after Letter I was published. This in turn raises a question about how closely Joseph was working with Oliver on these letters.

For example, one author wrote, "Surprisingly, it appears that Joseph was unaware of Oliver's intent to publicly document the history of the Church in the pages of the *Messenger and Advocate* until he read Oliver's statement in the October issue of his intention to do so."[27]

The only extant version of Joseph's letter is the undated one published in the December *Messenger and Advocate*. Consequently, we don't know when Joseph actually wrote it. The quotations in the letter, however, suggest Joseph was referring to an unpublished draft of the first number of the *Messenger and Advocate*, as well as a yet-unpublished Letter III.

Notice that Joseph's letter includes this passage, purportedly quoted from the first number of the paper: "give a history of the rise and progress of the church of the Latter Day Saints." But the version printed in the October *Messenger and Advocate* actually reads differently.

The following communication was designed to have been published in the last No. of the Star; but owing to a press of other matter it was laid over for this No. of the Messenger and Advocate. Since it was written, upon further reflection, **we have thought that a full history of the rise of the church of the Latter Day Saints**, and the most interesting parts **of its progress**, to the present time, would be worthy the perusal of the Saints. (emphasis added)

---

[27] Roger Nicholson examines this issue on page 31 in "The Cowdery Conundrum: Oliver's Aborted Attempt to Describe Joseph Smith's First Vision in 1834 and 1835," *Interpreter: A Journal of Mormon Scripture* 8 (2014): 27-44. Online at https://www.mormoninterpreter.com/the-cowdery-conundrum-olivers-aborted-attempt-to-describe-joseph-smiths-first-vision-in-1834-and-1835/. Nicholson proposes that Joseph was not ready to publish the First Vision but does not suggest a reason why. I proposed a reason in Chapter 8 of this book.

It is possible that Joseph was paraphrasing and simply misused the quotation marks, but why would he use quotation marks if he wasn't actually quoting the original article?

I think these quotation marks indicate that Joseph was quoting a pre-publication draft of Oliver's introduction to the letters. That is, an early draft read "history of the rise and progress of the Church" the way Joseph quoted it, but the published draft separated "progress" into the subsequent clause.

There is separate evidence that Joseph had access to early drafts of these letters. Joseph's letter includes a second quotation when it observes that the "history would necessarily embrace my life and character." Joseph quoted the phrase from Letter III—but Letter III was not published until December, when it appeared in the same issue as Joseph's letter.

Obviously, Joseph could not have taken this quotation from the very issue in which his letter appears. He had to have been privy to an unpublished draft of Letter III.

In Letter III, Oliver writes,

> You will recollect that I informed you, in my letter published in the first No. of the Messenger and Advocate, that **this history would necessarily embrace the life and character of our esteemed friend and brother, J. Smith JR.** one of the presidents of this church, and for information on that part of the subject, I refer you to his communication of the same, published in this paper. (emphasis added)

It is possible that Oliver adopted *Joseph's* phrase when he wrote Letter III, but that doesn't explain why Joseph put it in quotation marks.

Despite what Joseph wrote in his letter, Oliver's published Letter I does not use the word *character* or even refer to Joseph's *life*. Perhaps Oliver's original Letter I did refer to Joseph's "life and character," as Oliver mentions in Letter III, but if so, that portion of Letter I did not make it into print (or was moved to Letter III).

Months later, when Oliver wrote Letter VIII, he spent the last half of the letter discussing "the private life of one whose character has been so shamefully traduced." Perhaps the last half of Letter VIII was originally intended as an earlier letter, or even part of Letter I. In fact, this defense of the character of Joseph and his family was apparently a rebuttal to *Mormonism Unvailed* that would have made more sense in Letters I or II.

These details support the inference that in his letter, Joseph was referring to Oliver's pre-publication drafts of the history.

We would expect Joseph to have access to these drafts as Oliver explained in his introduction to the letters in October 1834.

> That our narrative may be correct, and particularly the introduction, it is proper to inform our patrons, that our brother J. SMITH jr. has offered to assist us. **Indeed, there are many items connected with the fore part of this subject that render his labor indispensable.** With his labor and with authentic documents now in our possession, we hope to render this a pleasing and agreeable narrative, well worth the examination and perusal of the Saints.- (emphasis added)

Oliver was not relying only on "authentic documents" or his personal knowledge, but on Joseph's "labor." What could that labor consist of other than reviewing the drafts of the letters?

The formality of Joseph writing a letter asking Oliver to publish it is consistent with a common practice of the day. Indeed, the historical letters themselves were nominally written in the form of private letters to W.W. Phelps, who was living in Missouri, even though they were obviously intended for publication.

A follow-up question is, if Joseph wrote the letter based on unpublished drafts and asked Oliver to publish it, why did Oliver wait until December to publish it?

A likely explanation is that Oliver wanted to first establish a context for Joseph's letter. Recall that *Mormonism Unvailed* was published in October 1834. That book was a direct attack on Joseph's character. Joseph's letter, on its own, could have been deemed an admission that the claims in *Mormonism Unvailed* were at least somewhat accurate.

Oliver avoided or at least mitigated this result by first publishing Letter II, in which he focuses on the humanity of past prophets and apostles.

Since the apostles fell asleep all men who profess a belief in the truth of their mission, extol their virtues and celebrate their fame. It seems to have been forgotten that they were men of infirmities and subject to all the feelings, passions, and imperfections common to other men. But it appears, that they, as others were before them, are looked upon as men of perfection, holiness, purity, and goodness, far in advance of any since.

Letter II doesn't even discuss Church history. Oliver seems to have written it purely to frame Joseph's letter, in which Joseph admits "many vices and follies" and writes:

it is not without a deep feeling of regret that I am thus called upon in answer to my own conscience, to fulfill a duty I owe to myself, as well as to the cause of truth, in making this public confession of my former uncircumspect walk, and unchaste conversation: and more particularly, as I often acted in violation of those holy precepts which I knew came from God.

Letter II puts Joseph's confession in an appropriate context by explaining that even the Biblical prophets were imperfect men. Letter II argues that expecting perfection in God's servants is unreasonable and unjustified.

Then Letter III resumes the history of the Church.

When Joseph's scribes copied Oliver's eight letters into *History, 1834-1836*, they omitted Joseph's letter to Oliver. They give no explanation for this choice.

When Benjamin Winchester published the collection of Oliver's letters in the *Gospel Reflector*, he placed Joseph's letter at the end, after Letter VIII. The Liverpool pamphlet, based on Winchester's version, did the same.

The version below is taken from the *Gospel Reflector*, 15 March 1842.

A LETTER FROM JOSEPH SMITH TO O. COWDERY.

Dear Brother, —

Having learned from the first No. of the Messenger and Advocate, that you were, not only about to "give a history of the rise and progress of the church of the Latter-Day Saints ;" but, that said "history would necessarily embrace my life and character," I have been induced to give you the time and place of my birth; as I have learned that many of the opposers of those principles which I have held forth to the world, profess a personal acquaintance with me, though when in my presence, represent me to be another person in age, education, and stature, from what I am.

I was born, (according to the record of the same, kept by my parents,) in the town of Sharon, Windsor Co. Vt. on the 23rd of December, 1805.

At the age of ten my father's family removed to Palmyra, N. Y. where, and in the vicinity of which, I lived, or, made it my place of residence, until I was twenty-one — the latter part, in the town of Manchester.

During this time, as is common to most; or all youths, I fell into many vices and follies ; but as my accusers are, and have been forward to accuse me of being guilty of gross and outrageous violations of the peace and good order of the community, I take the occasion to remark, that, though, as I have said above, "as is common to most, or all youths, I fell into many vices and follies," I have not, neither can it be sustained, in truth, been guilty of wronging or injuring any man or society of men ; and those imperfections to which I allude, and for which I have often had occasion to lament, were a light, and too often, vain mind, exhibiting a foolish and trifling conversation.

This being all, and the worst, that my accusers can substantiate against my moral character, I wish to add that it is not without a deep feeling of regret that I am thus called upon in answer to my own conscience, to fulfill a duty I owe to myself, as well as to the cause of truth, in making this public confession of my former uncircumspect walk, and trifling conversation: and more particularly, as I often acted in violation of those holy precepts which I knew came from God. But as the "Articles and Covenants," of this church are plain upon this particular point, I do not deem it important to proceed further. I only add, that I do not, nor never have, pretended to be any other than a man " subject to passion," and liable, without the assisting grace of the Saviour, to deviate from that perfect path in which all men are commanded to walk !

By giving the above a place in your valuable paper, you will confer a lasting favour upon myself, as an individual, and, as I humbly hope, subserve the cause of righteousness.

I am, with feelings of esteem, your fellow laborer in the Gospel of our Lord.

JOSEPH SMITH.

[Note: in the original, *Saviour* is spelled *Savior* and *favour* is spelled *favor*.]

Appendix III: Joseph Fielding Smith on Cumorah

Joseph Fielding Smith addressed the "Two-Cumorahs" question in 1936. Later, when he was President of the Quorum of the Twelve, his comments were republished in Joseph Fielding Smith, *Doctrines of Salvation*, comp. Bruce R. McConkie, 3:232–243.[28] I have placed the footnotes into the text in this extract and added emphasis in ***bold***.

WHERE IS THE HILL CUMORAH?

SPECULATION ABOUT BOOK OF MORMON GEOGRAPHY. Within recent years there has arisen among certain students of the Book of Mormon a theory to the effect that within the period covered by the Book of Mormon, the Nephites and Lamanites were confined almost entirely within the borders of the territory comprising Central America and the southern portion of Mexico-the isthmus of Tehauntepec probably being the "narrow neck" of land spoken of in the Book of Mormon rather than the isthmus of Panama. (Alma 50:34; 52:9; 63:5; Morm. 2:29; 3:5)...

LOCALE OF CUMORAH, RAMAH, AND RIPLIANCUM. This modernistic theory of necessity, in order to be consistent, must place the waters of Ripliancum and the Hill Cumorah some place within the

---

[28] The book is available online to subscribers at http://gospelink.com/library/document/1779. The discussion of Cumorah is also available online at http://emp.byui.edu/marrottr/cumorah-jfes-dofs3.pdf.

restricted territory of Central America, notwithstanding the teachings of the Church to the contrary for upwards of 100 years. *Because of this theory some members of the Church have become confused and greatly disturbed in their faith in the Book of Mormon.* It is for this reason that evidence is here presented to show that it is not only possible that these places could be located as the Church has held during the past century, but that in very deed such is the case.

It is known that the Hill Cumorah where the Nephites were destroyed is the hill where the Jaredites were also destroyed. This hill was known to the Jaredites as Ramah. It was approximately near to the waters of Ripliancum, which the Book of Ether says, "by interpretation, is large, or to exceed all." (Ether 15:8-11) Mormon adds: "And it came to pass that we did march forth to the land of Cumorah, and we did pitch our tents round about the hill Cumorah; and it was in a land of many waters, rivers, and fountains; and here we had hope to gain advantage over the Lamanites." (Morm. 6:4)

EARLY BRETHREN LOCATE CUMORAH IN WESTERN NEW YORK. *It must be conceded that this description fits perfectly the land of Cumorah in New York, as it has been known since the visitation of Moroni to the Prophet Joseph Smith, for the hill is in the proximity of the Great Lakes and also in the land of many rivers and fountains.* Moreover, the Prophet Joseph Smith himself is on record, definitely declaring the present hill called Cumorah to be the exact hill spoken of in the Book of Mormon. (History of the Church, 1948 ed., vol. 2, pp. 79-80.)

Further, the fact that all of his associates from the beginning down have spoken of it as the identical hill where Mormon and Moroni hid the records, must carry some weight. It is difficult for a reasonable person to believe that such men as Oliver Cowdery. Brigham Young, Parley P. Pratt, Orson Pratt, David Whitmer, and many others, could speak frequently of the Spot where the Prophet Joseph Smith obtained the plates as the Hill Cumorah, and not be corrected by the Prophet, if that were not the fact. That they did speak of this hill in the days of the Prophet in this definite manner is an established record of history.

OLIVER COWDERY PLACES CUMORAH IN WESTERN NEW YORK. The first reference of this kind is found in the *Messenger and Advocate*, a paper published by the Church in 1834-5. In a brief history of the rise of the Church prepared by Oliver Cowdery, he makes reference to this particular spot in the following words [quotes Letter VII]

PROPHET APPROVES OLIVER COWDERY'S VIEWS. *The quibbler might say that this statement from Oliver Cowdery is merely the opinion of Oliver Cowdery and not the expression of the Prophet Joseph Smith. It should be remembered that these letters in which these statements are made were written at the Prophet's request and under his personal supervision.* Surely, under these circumstances, he would not have permitted an error of this kind to creep into the record without correction.

At the commencement of these historical letters is found the following: "That our narrative may be correct, and particularly the introduction, it is proper to inform our patrons, that our Brother J. Smith Jr. . has offered to assist us. Indeed, there are many items connected with the fore part of this subject that render his labor indispensable. With his labor and with authentic documents now in our possession, we hope to render this a pleasing and agreeable narrative, well worth the examination and perusal of the saints." (M&A Oct., 1834, p. 13)

Later, during the Nauvoo period of the Church, and again under the direction of the Prophet Joseph Smith, these same letters by Oliver Cowdery, were published in the Times and Seasons, without any thought of correction had this description of the Hill Cumorah been an error. (*Times and Seasons*, Apr. 15, 1841, vol. 3, p. 379)

TESTIMONY OF DAVID WHITMER TO HILL CUMORAH.

Another testimony of interest is that of David Whitmer given to Elders Orson Pratt and Joseph F. Smith in September 1878, when they paid him a visit at his home in Richmond. To these brethren he said: "When I was returning to Fayette, with Joseph and Oliver, all of us riding in the wagon. Oliver and I on an old-fashioned wooden spring seat and Joseph behind us-while traveling along in a clear open space, a very pleasant, nice-looking old man suddenly appeared by the side of our wagon and saluted us with, 'Good morning, it is very warm,' at the same time wiping his face or forehead with his hand. We returned the salutation, and, by a sign from Joseph, I invited him to ride if he was going our way; but he said very pleasantly, 'No, I am going to Cumorah.' This name was something new to me; I did not know what Cumorah meant. We all gazed at him and at each other, and as I looked around inquiringly of Joseph, the old man instantly disappeared, so that I did not see him again."

Joseph F. Smith asked: "Did you notice his appearance?"

David Whitmer: "I should think I did. He was, I should think, about five feet eight or nine inches tall and heavy set.... His hair and beard were white, like Brother Pratt's, but his beard was not so heavy. I also remember that he had on his back a sort of knapsack with something in, shaped like a book." (Millennial Star, vol. 40, p. 772)

"GLAD TIDINGS FROM CUMORAH." Who can read the words of Joseph Smith as recorded in section 128:20 of the Doctrine and Covenants and not feel that he had reference to the Hill Cumorah in western New York?

While in this statement it is not positively declared that the Hill Cumorah is the place where the plates were obtained, yet the implication that such is the case is overwhelming.

JOSEPH SMITH LOCATES CUMORAH IN WESTERN NEW YORK. Perhaps this matter could rest at this point, but the question of the territory now embraced within the United States having been in possession of Nephites and Lamanites before the death of Mormon, carries some weight in the determining of this matter. In the light of revelation it is absurd for anyone to maintain that the Nephites and Lamanites did not possess this northern land. While Zion's camp was marching on the way to Jackson County, near the bank of the Illinois River they came to a mound containing the skeleton of a man. [Note: I omit the various accounts of Zelph's mound, where Joseph had a revelation during an excavation of a mound in Illinois. One account mentioned the East Sea in connection with Cumorah. Those interested in the details should consult Donald Q. Cannon's analysis of each description, available here: http://emp.byui.edu/marrottr/341folder/zelph%20revisited%20cannon.html]

ANCIENT CITY OF MANTI IN MISSOURI. The following is also taken from the history of the travels of the Kirtland Camp: "The camp passed through Huntsville, in Randolph County, which has been appointed as one of the stakes of Zion, and is the ancient site of the City of Manti, and pitched tents at Dark Creek, Salt Licks, seventeen miles...." (*Millennial Star*, vol. 16, p. 296)...

The following account of the same event is taken from the daily journal of the Kirtland Camp, and was written by Samuel D. Tyler: "September 25, 1838. We passed through Huntsville, Co, seat of Randolph Co .... There are several of the brethren round about here and this is the ancient site of the City of Manti, which is spoken of in the Book of Mormon and this is appointed one of the Stakes of Zion, and it is in Randolph County, Missouri, three miles west of the county seat." (Journal of Samuel D. Tyler, Sept. 25, 1838, filed in Church Historian's Office)

NEPHITE AND JAREDITE WARS IN WESTERN NEW YORK.

In the face of this evidence coming from the Prophet Joseph Smith, Oliver Cowdery, and David Whitmer, we cannot say that the Nephites and Lamanites did not possess the territory of the United States and that the Hill Cumorah is in Central America. Neither can we say that the great struggle which resulted in the destruction of the Nephites took place in Central America. If Zelph, a righteous man, was fighting under a great prophet-general in the last battles between the Nephites and Lamanites; if that great prophet-general was known from the Rocky Mountains to "the Hill Cumorah or eastern sea," then some of those battles, and evidently the final battles did take place within the borders of what is now the United States.

There were no righteous prophets, save the Three Nephites, after the death of Moroni, and we learn that Zelph was slain during one of these battles during the great last struggle between the Nephites and Lamanites and was buried near the Illinois River.

In the Book of Mormon story the Lamanites were constantly crowding the Nephites back towards the north and east. If the battles in which Zelph took part were fought in the country traversed by the Zion's Camp, then we have every reason to believe from what is written in the Book of Mormon, that the Nephites were forced farther and farther to the north and east until they found themselves in the land of Ripliancum, which both Ether and Mormon declare to us was the land of Ramah or Cumorah, a land of "many waters," which "by interpretation, is large, or to exceed all." (Ether 15:8-11)

This being true, what would be more natural then that Moroni, like his father Mormon, would deposit the plates in the land where the battles came to an end and the Nephites were destroyed? This Moroni says he did, and from all the evidence in the Book of Mormon, augmented by the testimony of the Prophet Joseph Smith, these final battles took place in the territory known as the United States and in the neighborhood of the Great Lakes and hills of Western New York. And here Moroni found the resting place for the sacred instruments which had been committed to his care. (Church News, Sept. 10, 1938, pp, 1, 6; reprinted. Feb. 27, 1954, pp. 2-3)

IMPRESSIONS AT CUMORAH

LORD LED PROPHET'S FAMILY TO CUMORAH-LAND. As I stood upon these sacred places I had peculiar feelings which I cannot describe. I always do have such feelings; I have visited the Hill Cumorah and the Sacred Grove on other occasions. As I stood at the Smith home, I thought of the early struggles of the family, and wondered what means the Lord might have used to get them to move from Vermont or New Hampshire, if they had not been forced from these states by poverty. Their poverty was not the result of indolence, as the wicked have proclaimed, but the poverty and reverses of Providence, sent to give experience and to lead the family to a better land where the Lord could perform his work through the youthful Seer, yet to be raised up....

CUMORAH ONCE SITE OF CARNAGE AND DESTRUCTION. As I stood upon the summit of the Hill Cumorah, in the midst of a vast multitude, only a few of whom belonged to the Church, I tried to picture the scenes of former days. Here were assembled vast armies filled with bitterness and bent on destruction. I thought of the great promises the Lord had made through his prophets concerning those who should possess this choice land, and how those promises were not fulfilled because the people violated his commandments. Here a people perished because of their extreme wickedness.

There must be something in the destiny of things that would cause a repetition of this terrible scene on the same spot many centuries later. I reflected and wondered if this unhappy time would ever come when another still mightier people would incur the wrath of God because of wickedness and likewise perish. If so, would this same spot witness their destruction? I thought of the prophets, Ether, Mormon, Moroni, and tried to realize the sadness of their feelings as they witnessed the mad onrushing of their peoples to annihilation.

IMPORTANCE OF CUMORAH UNKNOWN TO WORLD. (President attended a conference at the Joseph Smith Farm near Palmyra, New York, on Sept. 21 to 23, 1923—the 100th anniversary of the appearance of Moroni to Joseph Smith.)

Here it was that Moroni, commanded by the Lord, hid up the sacred records of his people. Here it was. 1,400 years later, that he, then a resurrected being, came to Joseph Smith and committed these same records to the young man's care. At the time of the Prophet's first visit to the hill, it was covered with trees; today (1923) it is stripped and bare, save for the grass which grows abundantly. This former scene of strife and bloodshed, where two nations perished, later the sacred repository of ancient records, today is the abode of peaceful cattle, reclining and chewing the cud. The many millions of inhabitants of the land, who, because they love darkness rather than light, will not believe, and although an angel has declared it unto them, they appear to have no more thought concerning the wonderful events that have taken place near and on the Hill Cumorah, than have these cattle. (20 Rel. Soc. Mag., vol. 10, pp. 586–587)

-→▷▷ ◁◁←-

Appendix IV: Cumorah and Book of Mormon Geography

The fact that Cumorah is in New York raises the question, does the text describe a North American setting?

I think it does.

An in-depth discussion of geography is beyond the scope of this book, but here is an overview of the map that I explain in more detail in *Moroni's America*.

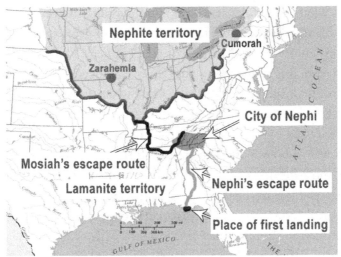

But I recognize there is plenty of room for different interpretations—including a Mesoamerican setting with Cumorah in New York.

I encourage you to study the issues and make up your own mind.

About the Author

For decades, I accepted what I had been taught in seminary and at BYU: the Book of Mormon took place in Central America (Mesoamerica). I studied books and articles published by FARMS, the Maxwell Institute, *BYU Studies*, and other LDS publishers. I visited sites in Central America, attended symposiums, and discussed the issues with a variety of experts. But Cumorah in Mexico didn't make sense.

Eventually I concluded that the Mesoamerican theory of Book of Mormon geography doesn't match the text, doesn't fit real-world geology, anthropology, or archaeology, and, most importantly, doesn't align with what Church leaders have taught about Cumorah.

When I learned about the Heartland theory of geography, it seemed more congruent with the teachings of the prophets. That was good enough for me, but as a lawyer (like Oliver Cowdery), I believe truth also emerges from consideration of all the facts, when assessed with sound logic. My CES teachers had never told me about Letter VII. When I read it I was impressed by Oliver's confidence in the *fact* (as he put it) that Cumorah was in New York. I re-examined the text and discovered that Mormon and Moroni were describing *North America*—from New York to Missouri to Florida. That's what led me to write *Moroni's America*.

Later, I realized that Joseph translated two separate sets of plates, as briefly outlined in the timelines in this book. This means the plates of Nephi (D&C 10, now 1 Nephi through Words of Mormon) came from Mormon's depository in the hill Cumorah in New York. This further corroborated President Cowdery's statements in Letter VII. This is explained in detail in *Whatever Happened to the Golden Plates?*

If you accept the Mesoamerican theory despite Letter VII, I hope reading this book helps you appreciate other perspectives as we all seek to bring people unto Christ through the Book of Mormon

Jonathan Neville April 2018

Made in the USA
Las Vegas, NV
26 February 2023

68179328R00085